Cleveland Amusement Park Memories

A Nostalgic Look Back at
Euclid Beach Park • Puritas Springs Park
Geauga Lake Park • and Other Classic Parks

David and Diane Francis

GRAY & COMPANY, PUBLISHERS
CLEVELAND

Gray & Company, Publishers
1588 E. 40th St.
Cleveland, OH 44103

Library of Congress Cataloging-in-Publication Data
Francis, David W., 1947-
Cleveland amusement park memories / by David and Diane Francis.
p. cm.
1. Amusement parks—Ohio—Cleveland—History. I. Francis, Diane DeMali, 1945-
II. Title.
GV1853.3.O3F73 2004
791'.06'80977132—dc22   2004022253
ISBN 1-886228-89-2

Contents

Introduction

Paul Boyton's Water Chutes Park, the world's first amusement park, debuted in Chicago, Illinois, in 1894. Tracing its origins to such early pleasures as the picnic grove, the seaside summer resort, and the 1893 World's Fair Midway Plaisance, the amusement park quickly became the world's newest entertainment darling. Indeed, offering much more than just one diversion, the amusement park delighted patrons with an often dizzying mixture of sensory delights. Situated within a single area one might enjoy thrilling mechanical rides, delicious foods, challenging games, vaudeville, concerts, roller-skating, dancing, swimming, bowling, hotels, moving pictures, animal shows, shopping, and more. In short, the amusement park offered what had never been available before: an all-inclusive public venue featuring nearly every kind of entertainment.

The amusement park was born into a briskly expanding family of leisure-time entertainments for the masses.

Its siblings included the modern-day circus, the carnival, burlesque, vaudeville, dance halls, roller-skating rinks, and moving pictures. This era of burgeoning commercial entertainments lasted from the 1880s to the 1920s. Leaders of the movement were canny enough to see the potential for huge profits to be made by courting America's rapidly emerging middle class. Shorter workweeks, more disposable income, new developments in both intercity and intracity transportation, technological advances in electricity, and the desire to cement relations between management and labor made commercial recreation for the average family possible and profitable.

An exciting, never-before-seen entertainment form, amusement parks appeared in rapid succession in cities and towns all across America. By 1912, Ohio was home to 54 amusement parks and dozens of picnic groves. New York had 62 parks, Pennsylvania's population supported 61, and Massachusetts followed with 38. Even sparsely populated Montana could boast of four amusement parks. While amusement parks were built along the seaside, on the shores of rivers and lakes, and even in small towns, it was the large population centers that offered entrepreneurs the most promising opportunity for huge profits. Chicago, the birthplace of the modern amusement park, was home to no fewer than eight amusement parks before 1920. These included Chutes Park (1894–1907), Ferris Wheel Park (1896–1902), Sans Souci Park (1899–1929), White City (1904–1934), Riverview Park (1904–1967), Luna Park (1908–1911), Forest Park (1908–1923), and Cream City Park (1911–1917). Riverview Park was one of America's largest and finest parks and compared favorably with Cleveland's Euclid Beach Park.

The amusement park construction craze hit full stride about 1905, the year Cleveland's Luna Park debuted. New parks continued to appear until the 1920s, but by the time of the First World War, the novelty had worn thin and the phenomenal growth of the park industry was tapering off. The park market was saturated. Parks began to lose their luster for the once-bedazzled patrons. By the late 1920s, numerous amusement parks were closing their gates, while others struggled mightily to survive. The Great Depression and the demise of the electric railways that had owned and served scores of parks were two contributing factors. Only the strongest parks survived the 1930s and the material shortages of the ensuing war years.

Even those parks that survived the Great Depression and the privations of World War II did not enjoy clear sailing into the postwar era. To be sure, the postwar baby boom provided a much-needed boost for the industry. However, rising insurance and labor costs, the burden of maintaining old amusement rides, and competition from other entertainment venues thinned profit margins. In addition, the owners of urban parks faced the threat of civil disturbances and racial confrontations. As land values soared, many park owners were content to sell their parks to real estate developers. The decade of the 1960s was particularly tragic for some of the nation's grand old amusement parks. Forest Park Highlands in St. Louis was destroyed by fire in 1963, Coney Island's Steeplechase Park closed in 1964, Chicago's Riverview Park in 1967, and Cleveland's beloved Euclid Beach Park in 1969. New Jersey's legendary Palisades Park held out until 1972.

In the mid-1890s, Cleveland and the rest of northern Ohio were ripe for amusement park development. A Great Lakes port blessed with rapid industrialization, Cleveland became the largest city in Ohio and the nation's sixth-largest urban center. Under the leadership of Mayor Tom L. Johnson, the city's electric street railway system evolved into a model operation and provided the transportation so vital for the development of amusement parks. While both Forest City Park and Washington Park had carousels and a few other attractions, Euclid Beach Park has the distinction of being Cleveland's first real amusement park. Opening in 1895, just one year after the debut of Chicago's Chutes Park, Euclid Beach was located well east of the city and was connected to the population center by the steamships *Duluth* and *Superior*. Acquired by the Humphrey family in 1901, Euclid Beach Park would become revered as a paragon of family entertainment, a leader in ride technology, and the envy of most park operators. Although Puritas Springs Park opened on the west side of Cleveland in 1898, Euclid Beach suffered no real competition until 1905, when Pittsburgh amusement park and ride builder Frederick Ingersoll constructed Luna Park on Cleveland's east side. The spectacular new attraction quickly became Cleveland's favorite amusement center, overshadowing Euclid Beach. Whereas Euclid Beach had been "dry" since the Humphrey takeover in 1901, a healthy portion of Luna Park's profits came from the sale of alcoholic beverages. Consequently, when Prohibition made the sale of liquor illegal in 1919, Luna began a decade-long downward spiral that ended with the abrupt closing of the park in 1929. By this time, Euclid Beach had far outdistanced Luna and had reemerged as Cleveland's premier park.

Puritas Springs closed in 1958 and Euclid Beach followed suit eleven years later. Of all the Cleveland-area parks, only Memphis Kiddie Park (opened in 1952) and Geauga Lake Park (located in Aurora) remained. The latter was purchased by a group of former Cedar Point executives and evolved into a modern "Super Park," eventually becoming part of the Six Flags chain. In the spring of 2004 the facility was rechristened Geauga Lake after it was sold to Cedar Fair, owner of Cedar Point in Sandusky, Ohio, as well as a number of other amusement parks around the country.

From this distance, it's easy to view Cleveland's early amusement parks as mere footnotes in social and economic history. But they are so much more than that. For more than seventy-five years these boisterous, colorful, exciting meccas fulfilled the fantasies of entertainment-hungry Clevelanders. Each park had its own distinct personality, its own peculiarities, and its own alluring array of popular attractions. Each park had its own unique smells. At Euclid Beach it was the stately sycamores and the unforgettable odor of the lake and of damp earth beneath the pier. Luna enticed customers with the smell of warm melt-in-your-mouth waffles, and at Puritas Springs the odor of warm oil on the chain of the Cyclone coaster signaled a thrilling ride. And of course there were the sounds. The chatter of Monkey Island at Luna Park, the sharp reports of the Shooting Gallery at Geauga Lake, the splash of a boat at the end of White City's Shoot-the-Chutes, and the ever-present levity of Laughing Sal at Euclid Beach's Surprise House. And let's not forget the music. There was Liberati's na-

tionally known band at Luna Park; a smaller concert band at White City, and the giant Gavioli band organ in the Skating Rink at Euclid Beach. In dimly lit ballrooms couples swayed to dance bands; whirling carousel menageries were accompanied by band organs; in the vaudeville theaters stage bands entertained; and on the midways military bands added to the unique amusement park cacophony.

More than just business establishments, the parks were sights, and sounds, and smells. Moreover, they were the birthplace of treasured memories for children and adults alike. It is the hope of the authors that the following pages will re-create the park atmospheres in which these memories were born. For those who never visited these parks, let the imagination run wild and enjoy the parks that thrilled your parents, grandparents, and great-grandparents. And for those who remember Euclid Beach, Puritas Springs, or old Geauga Lake Park, we hope you enjoy this scenic excursion into the past.

KIDDIE
FERRIS WHEEL
ONE
TICKET.

Euclid Beach Park

In 1924, the Humphreys used their concrete-pouring system to create the large Colonnade building. That same season they began building a Kiddie Land in the Colonnade. One of the first rides installed was the Kiddie Ferris Wheel.

After 1901, when it was purchased by the Humphrey family, Euclid Beach became what was known as a "Sunday School" operation. The Humphrey Company imposed strict rules of deportment on park guests and established a code of decency that set Euclid Beach apart from most other parks in the industry.

Alcoholic beverages were not sold at Euclid Beach, nor were they permitted on park grounds; and any person who was obviously under the influence of alcohol was turned away at the gate. The Humphreys had no tolerance for rowdy behavior of any kind, and they employed their own police to enforce park rules. Games of chance found no home at Euclid Beach, which, unlike many northern Ohio parks, never installed illegal slot machines. While Luna Park thrived by presenting sensational and titillating shows, the Humphrey Company turned its back on any entertainments that hinted at sexuality or were in any way gruesome or in bad taste. Euclid Beach went so far as to advertise that it would present nothing that would demoralize or depress and that park patrons would never be exposed to undesirable people.

By the 1920s, Dudley S. Humphrey II was acknowledged by his peers as one of America's leading amusement managers. Despite this praise, few parks followed Humphrey's policies and many park men criticized his methods. Most parks painted their buildings either a pristine white or some vivid, attention-getting color. In stark contrast, the Humphreys painted their park in a drab green that

became known in the park industry as "Humphrey Green." Parker Beach, the owner of Chippewa Lake Park, joked that "old Dud Humphrey bought a million gallons of that paint in 1910 and they're still using it."

Dudley Humphrey also introduced the controversial Humphrey Park Plan at Euclid Beach. Developed as a method of maintaining tighter cash control, the Humphrey Park Plan required that patrons purchase tickets that were then used for rides, food, and even souvenirs. Cash was accepted only at the penny arcade and the lakeside restaurant. Robert McKay, manager of Buckeye Lake Park, recalled, "The Humphreys never seemed to understand that rather than stealing cash, they [the employees] 'palmed' tickets and gave them to their family and friends." Whatever the shortcomings of the Park Plan, the company sold tickets by the millions. In 1920, a postwar recession year with high unemployment, 22,488,602 tickets were dispensed to eager patrons.

The Humphreys also had some unique ideas regarding amusement park foods. Popcorn, popcorn balls, and candy kisses (a type of taffy offered in just one flavor) were the mainstay of Euclid Beach's food service. To keep the park supplied, the Humphreys started growing their own popping corn in 1927. Peanuts were roasted and sold for a number of years; and, after the Kohr Brothers invented soft-serve ice cream in 1919, Frozen Whip was offered—again, like the candy kisses, in just one flavor. For many years, the park's beverage selection was

limited to Vernor's Ginger Ale, Hires Root Beer, and Phez Loganberry Juice. The park restaurant served a limited lunch and dinner menu, while the Main Lunch, near the Aero Dips roller coaster, offered hot dogs, boiled ham sandwiches, pies, doughnuts, and coffee. The more traditional park fare such as hamburgers, French fries, cotton candy, waffles, and candy apples didn't appear at Euclid Beach until its last years of operation. But, even though the Humphreys stubbornly refused

At the head of the Humphrey Company was Dudley Sherman Humphrey II. Many amusement park operators considered his methods unorthodox, but they could not argue with success. Just before his death in 1933, *Amusement Park Management* magazine devoted an entire issue to Humphrey and the park he built.

☞ By 1910, the average American consumed nearly eighty pounds of sugar per year. Little wonder that Humphrey's Candy Kisses were so popular with generations of Clevelanders. On the second floor, the candy is being pulled prior to being cut to size, individually wrapped, and packaged for sale.

Loganberry juice was a popular beverage at Euclid Beach for many years. When it was discovered that the juice could ferment in warm weather, however, the very ethical park management quickly stopped serving it.

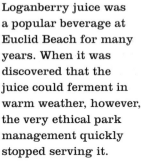

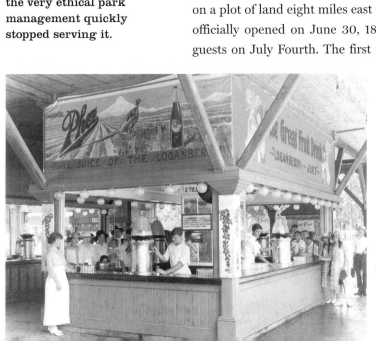

to change their food policy, few could argue with their success. In 1942, the park sold 58,467 pounds of hot dogs, or about 600,000 servings! Two seasons later, Euclid Beach patrons ate 8,329 pounds of boiled ham, 24,890 pounds of roasted peanuts, 10,540 pies, 112,404 doughnuts, and 243,000 boxes of popcorn, proving that hungry park visitors will eat whatever they're offered.

While the Humphrey family was single-handedly responsible for the success of Euclid Beach, they neither conceived nor built the original operation. The Euclid Beach Park Company was formed in 1894, and soon after, construction began on a plot of land eight miles east of Cleveland's Public Square. The lakeside park officially opened on June 30, 1895, and reportedly entertained fifty thousand guests on July Fourth. The first manager, William R. Ryan, supervised a fairly small operation that included the new Dance Pavilion, a beer garden, and some shows. The park's early drawing card was music. Jessie Hammerstrom, who was born in 1889 and visited the embryonic park, recalled that "Everyone went to Euclid Beach to dance and to listen to concert bands. They didn't have many rides in those days." Dancing was offered in the large ballroom, but concert bands were the biggest attraction. Ryan booked some major bands, including the nationally famous band

I REMEMBER . . . We lived right in the park by the parking lot and where the bowling alley used to be. It was also very near the back turn of the Thriller, and as I went to bed at night I could hear the people screaming as the Thriller train came around the back turn. If the wind blew properly, I could also hear the organ music playing from underneath the Rocket Ships.

Wintertime was fun in the park. My cousin lived on the east side near the mobile home park, and we had friends who lived in the mobile homes. We'd play wonderful cops and robbers games in the park. We would also ride our bikes all around the park. That was a lot of fun until my cousin fell off her bike, broke her arm, and my dad put a stop to that.

We would explore the Laff in the Dark and walk through the closed ride. One of my great ideas was to take a sled down the Flying Turns, which luckily did not work because the lower parts of the ride never got covered with snow. I later learned that David Scott, my first cousin once removed and son of the park engineer, used to ride a bike down the Flying Turns. I wished I had thought of that!

I did work at the park. The park closed when I was nineteen, so I had all sorts of mundane jobs. I cut grass a lot, I ran the garbage truck a bit, I ran rides when I was old enough.

I got to know the carpenters who worked on the roller coasters, and when I was seven or eight years old I would climb up the coasters to visit them while they were working. I had a great time up there, but it is lucky my folks did not find out about it.

One thing I did not like was Laughing Sal, and when I was little I was scared of her. Some kids loved her. They would stand in front of her and laugh with her. There was no in-between, either you loved her and laughed with her or you hated her and tried not to get near her. I was in that other bunch.

It was a lot of fun. I didn't know how good I had it.

— *Dudley S. Humphrey, Jr.*

Euclid Beach's second roller coaster, the Figure Eight Roller Toboggan, was unveiled when the 1904 season opened. Built by the Philadelphia Toboggan Company, the coaster was small, relatively slow, and outdated within a few years. The Humphreys only operated the Figure 8 for five seasons.

Every early amusement park was home to at least one theater for vaudeville shows, band concerts, and various shows. Euclid Beach had two theaters, the Avenue Theatre and the wonderfully elaborate World Theatre (above).

One of the most unique carousels ever built was the Flying Ponies, installed at the Beach in 1903. Sometimes called the Japanese Flying Ponies (although built at North Tonawanda, New York), the horses were suspended in order to permit them to swing freely and operated at a steep angle. The ride remained at the park until about 1938.

of Frederick N. Innes. A virtuoso trombonist who was often compared to Arthur Pryor, Innes fronted one of America's finest "business bands." So popular was Euclid Beach in band circles that in 1897, H. Clark Thayer composed the "Euclid Beach Park March" in honor of the park. Thayer was the founder of Thayer's Military Band in Canton and was also a personal friend of President William McKinley, thus gaining his band the nickname "McKinley's Own."

During the infant park's second season, it evolved into a full-fledged amusement facility. Park manager Ryan contracted with LaMarcus A. Thompson to build the park's first roller coaster, the Switchback Railway. Thompson, a native Ohioan, designed and constructed the world's first roller coaster at Coney Island in 1884 and went on to become one of the most prolific manufacturers of Switchback Railways, Scenic Railways, and complete amusement parks. His Euclid Beach ride, which operated until 1903, was just 35 feet tall and 350 feet long, but it was the first roller coaster that most Clevelanders had ever seen. The 1896 season saw the introduction of a carousel, an observation wheel, and the Crystal Maze, an early walk-through fun house.

Since the park was located so far from downtown Cleveland, the company had a park pier built, purchased two 98-foot passenger steamships, *Duluth* and *Superior*, and initiated service from Cuyahoga River docks to the park. A round trip on the 800-passenger steamers cost 25 cents, which included admission to the park grounds. On days when management expected crowds of 25,000 or more, they chartered the steamers *State of Ohio* or *Promise* to assist the regular vessels. Steamship service to Euclid Beach lasted only through the 1900 season, and it was discontinued by the Humphrey Company when they took over in 1901.

As Euclid Beach added rides, shows, and a vaudeville theater, word of the park's pleasant lakeside offerings spread well beyond Cleveland. On July 27, 1898, the Medina Businessmen's Picnic and the A. I. Root Company chartered trains to take them to Cleveland, where they boarded the steamships for the trip to the park's pier. Although the Medina Businessmen's

One of the early amusement rides at Euclid Beach was the Witching Waves. The first ride of this type was installed at Coney Island's Luna Park in 1907. The inventor of the Witching Waves, Theopilus Van Kannel, is best remembered for inventing the revolving door in 1888.

The little steamships affectionately called the "Euclid Beach Tubs" operated between downtown Cleveland and the park from 1895 through the 1900 season.

The Circle Swing was the invention of Harry Traver, a prolific amusement ride designer. The Euclid Beach Circle Swing was erected overlooking the lake in 1902. The original airship cars were replaced with biplane cars and, finally, with the famous stainless-steel rocket cars during the 1930s.

Operating a miniature steam locomotive during the early 1900s was a hot and dirty job. Along with the roller coaster and the carousel, however, customers expected the diminutive railroads at every park.

I REMEMBER . . . I was born in 1889 and remember going to Euclid Beach and Scenic Park before 1900. In 1909, we went to Cedar Point on the steamship Eastland. I got very seasick on the trip back.

My brother owned the BAB Cigar Co. in Cleveland, and we all worked for him preparing tobacco to be rolled into cigars. On weekends we went to Scenic Park, Euclid Beach, White City, and Luna Park. Streetcars ran right up to the gate of Euclid Beach.

Euclid Beach popcorn balls were delicious. My sisters and I would buy some and sit on a bench near the lake to eat them. We always took a few home.

I remember they had an ostrich farm at the Beach when I was young.

Euclid Beach never changed much. It was always a nice place to go. — *Jessie Hammerstrom (1889–1983)*

group had previously patronized Chippewa Lake Park, Silver Lake, and Cedar Point, curiosity about Euclid Beach enticed them to visit the new Cleveland lakeside resort. Round-trip steamship fare was just 65 cents for adults and 35 cents for children and included admission to the park. A full day of music, games, and amusements was promised, but attendees were duly warned that ". . . the last boat leaves the park at 8 P.M." Thanks to favorable word of mouth, it wasn't long before picnic groups were traveling to Euclid Beach from other cities, including Ashland, Mansfield, and Akron.

Before they bought Euclid Beach, the Humphrey Company, operator of popcorn stands in Cleveland, was one of the park's early concessionaires. By 1899 the Humphreys had become disillusioned by the sale of alcohol, the rowdy behavior, and the objectionable shows at "the Beach," and they closed their Euclid Beach popcorn stand. However, when the Euclid Beach Park Company failed after the 1900 season, the Humphreys moved quickly to acquire the property and institute their own ideas of park management. The new owners eliminated the gate charges, negotiated a one-fare price on streetcars to the park, replaced unacceptable concessions, and terminated the sale of beer. In addition, they publicly announced that any rowdy, intoxicated, or undesirable patrons would be denied admission or removed from the park.

The Humphrey formula worked. With some exaggera-

The Custer Specialty Company installed the prototype of their new ride, the Zoomer, at Euclid Beach during the late 1920s. The Zoomer not only failed to provide any thrills, but, as longtime park employee Walter Williams recalled, the propellers killed insects and deposited them on the faces of the riders. The ride lasted only a few seasons.

☞

Camping was offered at Euclid Beach from the earliest seasons. In 1907, $40,000 was invested in the Camp Grounds, and campers could rent tents with one, two, three, four, or five rooms. Even in the 1950s, a four-room tent could be rented for four dollars a day.

The Humphrey Company developed a system for pouring structural concrete that was used throughout the park. In 1915, the company constructed a number of concrete cottages that could be rented by the season. Many of these sturdy cottages were still in existence long after the park closed in 1969.

tion, Dudley Humphrey announced that 1,500,000 people passed through the Euclid Beach Park gates during the 1901 season; and the popcorn stand alone registered sales of $10,000 (before 1899, annual popcorn sales at the park never exceeded $2,000). The stage was set, and the foresighted Humphrey family was poised to build Euclid Beach into one of America's finest and most respected amusement parks.

With a successful season behind them, the Humphreys embarked on a major expansion plan for the 1902 season. Harry Traver's new amusement ride, the Circle Swing, was purchased and installed near the lake (this ride later became the Rocket Ships and operated until the park closed in 1969). The World Theatre also opened that season, as did the rustic Log Cabin building. The Log Cabin started life as the Forestry Building at the 1901 Pan-American Exposition in Buffalo. After the World's Fair closed, the Humphreys bought and disassembled the structure, spending $17,248 to reconstruct it as the Log Cabin at the park.

The Scenic Railway was the third roller coaster to rise over the park's landscape. This large coaster, with its distinctive station building, opened in 1907 and operated until 1936. Note the traditional Euclid Beach ticket booth, which was still in use when the park closed in 1969.

After 1902, park improvements came at a rapid pace. In 1903, the Flying Ponies were installed, followed in 1904 by the Roller Skating Rink and a Figure Eight roller coaster from the Philadelphia Toboggan Company. A year later, the same company sold the park a new carousel (which was replaced in 1910 by a larger and more elaborate Philadelphia Toboggan carousel that resided at the park until 1969).

It was soon obvious that the Humphrey Company would build Euclid Beach around the "Queen of the Midway," the roller coaster. With the old Switchback

The Aero Dips coaster began life in 1909 as the New Velvet Coaster. For thousands of Clevelanders, the mild Aero Dips provided an introduction to coasters before they graduated to the more intense Thriller, Racing Coaster, and Flying Turns. The Aero Dips was razed in 1964.

Space was always in short supply in amusement parks, and managers tried to make the best use of the available ground. Here, the wooden track of the Red Bug Boulevard winds through the structure of the Racing Coaster.

Railway razed and the Figure Eight operating, they sought out the latest and most exciting advancements in roller coaster engineering. In 1907, Euclid Beach made its largest investment to date. LaMarcus A. Thompson was recruited to design Euclid Beach's Scenic Railway at a cost of $38,670.17. Large and impressive, the Scenic Railway included darkened tunnels that were particularly popular with young couples. Two years later, America's greatest coaster engineer, John A. Miller of Homewood, Illinois, was engaged to design and build the New Velvet Coaster next to the Skating Rink. Later renamed the Aero Dips, this somewhat modest and mild coaster became a favorite with several generations of Clevelanders. Then, in 1913, while Miller was chief engineer for the Ingersoll Engineering & Construction Company, he conceived one of the park's signature attractions, the Racing Coaster. Originally known as the Derby Racer, this huge coaster cost $44,195 to build; but by carrying 72 riders per trip, it quickly paid for itself. In July 1951, for example, the Racing Coaster entertained 80,126 riders.

Euclid Beach grew throughout the 1910s. Crowds increased dramatically, and the Humphreys continued to add rides and attractions that fit their plans for an amusement park. In 1918, the park sold 11,906,866 tickets, while the company

The Flying Turns, opened in 1930, was the last coaster constructed at Euclid Beach. Invented by First World War aviator J. Norman Bartlett, the Flying Turns was a breathtakingly fast ride that combined the thrills of flying and bobsledding. This was the largest Flying Turns ride ever built.

During the early decades of the twentieth century, there were 100,000 soda fountains in the United States, and Americans spent $500 million a year on carbonated beverages. The Soda Grill at Euclid Beach offered a variety of sodas and sundaes, as well as fresh-squeezed orangeade, lemonade, and limeade.

payroll climbed to $101,089. A year later, ticket sales soared to 16,706,605, and payroll increased again by about 20 percent. All of this was accomplished in the face of stiff competition from a powerful rival: Cleveland's Luna Park.

The postwar recession of 1920–21 appears to have had little impact on Euclid Beach as ticket sales and attendance continued to climb. The 1920s, however, were a decade of uneven prosperity. After reaching 22 million in 1920, Euclid Beach ticket sales fell to 13,666,454 in 1929. At the Skating Rink, attendance slipped from 90,549 in 1925 to 80,329 two seasons later. Nevertheless, the Humphrey Company continued to expand the park each season. A Mill Chute (later rebuilt as Over the Falls) was installed in 1920, followed by the landmark Thriller roller coaster. A new Dodgem was added, Kiddieland was expanded, the Bug was purchased from the Traver Engineering Company, and finally, the magnificent Flying Turns was added to greet park visitors when the 1930 season opened.

By the time the Flying Turns debuted, the entire amusement industry was feeling the impact of the Great Depression. Amusement parks, already declin-

☞

Helium-filled balloons were always treasured souvenirs of a visit to Euclid Beach, despite their short life. During 1932, a dismal economic year, the park sold 17,000 balloons. By 1937, with the economy improving, balloon sales increased to 44,000; in 1949, the number reached 66,000.

After the Sea Swing ride was removed from a circular cement pool, a wading pool was created with a magnificent fountain at the center. At night, the flowing water was illuminated by colored lights. In the background is the park's famous pier, a favorite place for fishing or just strolling.

The Kiddie Cars were a smaller version of the Red Bug Boulevard that operated near the Racing Coaster. Rides that simulated automobiles were immensely popular with children during the 1920s and 1930s.

ing in popularity, were devastated by the Depression. Of small consolation was the fact that most of the commercial recreation industry suffered the same fate. Movie theaters reported a decline of 25 million patrons per week, and some radio stations switched off their transmitters. Circuses folded their tents, carnivals attempted to sell their rides, and summer resort hotels were nearly empty. By 1930, 72 percent of America's amusement parks reported significant declines in revenue. Just a year later, the number of parks affected increased to 85 percent. Between 1929 and 1930, parks lost 41 percent of their group picnic business. In 1931, Cincinnati's well-managed Coney Island Park reported attendance figures that showed a 13 percent decline; also that year, Cedar Point's parent, the G. A. Boeck-

ling Company, recorded the last profit it would see for twenty years.

No matter how well run Euclid Beach was it could not cope with the effects of the worldwide depression. Ticket sales at Euclid Beach told the entire story. From 11,300,979 tickets sold in 1930, sales plummeted to 5,869,654 in 1933 (just 26 percent of the sales it had enjoyed in 1920). Grudgingly, the company learned to operate with fewer employees. The annual payroll fell from $233,488 in 1930 to $82,957 three years later.

Admission to the Skating Rink was reduced to 40 cents, but the flow of eager roller skaters had been reduced by 50 percent, and it seemed that nothing could be done to increase ticket sales. To add to the park's troubles, founder Dudley S. Humphrey II died on September 7, 1933. It was left to Harvey, his son, to take over the reins of the park at the worst possible time.

Built in 1921 by the California firm of Prior & Church, the Great American Racing Derby was one of the unique rides that made Euclid Beach special. The speedy horse race ride was sold to Cedar Point, where it still operates as Cedar Downs.

Euclid Beach's original Kiddieland carousel was built by the Philadelphia Toboggan Company and installed in the Colonnade near other miniaturized rides. The carousel mounted a variety of small animals in addition to horses. When these other animals proved frightening or unpopular with the children, an all-horse carousel replaced the ride.

The centerpiece of the Skating Rink was the mammoth band organ built about 1900 by Gavioli of Paris. It originally played at the Elysium, an ice-skating rink owned by the Humphrey Company, but was moved to Euclid Beach in 1910. The Rink entertained 90,549 roller skaters in 1925, but thereafter attendance declined to just 29,232 in 1947. The Skating Rink was finally closed in 1962.

I REMEMBER . . . Having grown up in the East 116th and Harvard Avenue area of Cleveland, I was sort of equidistant from Euclid Beach and Geauga Lake Park. Since I wasn't really close to either of them, I would only get to go to them on special occasions such as school or factory picnics. Having relatives in the house that worked at the White Motor Company and Ohio Forge (and my mom at Leece Neville Company), I had the chance to go to the parks at least three times a year. Over the years the companies held their shop picnics at various parks. Another opportunity afforded itself when the schools held their annual school picnic at Euclid Beach.

Of the two parks, Euclid Beach had to be my favorite. It was the biggest, and had the most roller coasters and other rides. I can remember as a youngster going into the fun house with my mother, Sophie Szuch, and being so scared of things popping out at me that I closed my eyes and buried them in her skirt as I hung on for dear life.

I can also remember standing and watching the Flying Turns ride, which was my favorite coaster at the park. As the cars would go through the course you could see the whole structure sway from the weight of the cars going up the sides of the barrel-like course! I always waited for the structure to collapse, but it didn't stop me from going on it.

Another favorite ride was the Rocket Ships. Having grown up in the 1940s, Buck Rogers and Flash Gordon were favorite comic strips of mine, and when those sleek chrome-covered rocket ships soared outward you felt as though you were Buck or Flash. Not too many years ago I saw one of those

The Kiddie Boat Ride, known in the park industry as a "Wet Boat," was another ride installed in the Colonnade to serve the ever-increasing numbers of baby boom children visiting Euclid Beach.

rocket ships that someone had converted into a motor vehicle and was driving south in on Interstate 271. I was exiting onto Interstate 480 West when I looked over and saw it go by. I almost went off the road because I was so excited.

Probably my most favorite ride at Euclid Beach was the Sleepy Hollow Railroad. It was undoubtedly the slowest ride in the park, but I just loved it when it went past the miniature village with its houses and vehicles. When the park closed, I believe that was the ride I missed the most.

My other personal favorite place at the park was the Penny Arcade. It was truly named because for a penny you could go in and play the claw machines to try to pick up prizes (that often were too heavy for the claw to hold) or collect the exhibit cards of movies, baseball, football, pinups, and other subjects. I always came home

The postwar Baby Boom prompted Euclid Beach to expand Kiddieland even more. In 1949, the Kiddie Mill Chute was built behind the Colonnade. Gentle and equipped with a very small hill, the ride was a child's version of the much larger Over the Falls ride.

A perennial favorite at Euclid Beach until the park closed in 1969 was the Flying Scooters ride. Built by Chicago's Bisch-Rocco Amusement Company, it was purchased in 1938 and placed in front of the Colonnade.

with a stack of them and still have a number of them some fifty years later. Same goes for the "Chinese Finger Traps"—I'm sure I still have one buried away in an old cigar box.

You also cannot forget the eating treats. A trip to the park was not complete without eating custard ice cream in a sugar cone, popcorn balls, Belgian waffles with powdered sugar, and, of course, taffy. I remember standing there watching the taffy machines with the arms rotating as they stretched the taffy out before cutting it into nuggets and individually wrapping them.

On the trip to Euclid Beach, I would always look for the Commodore movie theater, followed shortly by the ice-cream stand on the south side of Lakeshore Boulevard. The ice-cream stand was built like an inverted sugar cone, and I knew that once I saw that we were close to the park. — *John F. Szuch*

By the later 1930s, the 1927 biplane cars on the Circle Swing were becoming very outdated. The park's maintenance department designed and built three new large, stainless-steel rockets. The name of the ride was changed from the Airplanes to the Rocket Ships, and it remained a favorite until closing day.

Surprisingly, rather than hibernate during the difficult years of the 1930s, the Humphrey Company forged ahead. Euclid Beach Park was maintained in first-rate condition, and a few new rides were even added. Euclid Beach never built another roller coaster, but it continually expanded and upgraded in other areas. A number of sensibly priced kiddie rides were purchased, and in 1935 the Surprise House fun house was added. Skee Ball alleys were installed along with a new Shooting Gallery. When the worst of the Depression had passed, new major rides began to appear: Cuddle Up (1937), Dippy Whip and Flying Scooters (1938), and Bubble Bounce (1939).

After the Second World War, the Humphrey family attempted to modernize Euclid Beach. Two expensive additions were the Antique Cars in the old Skating Rink and the Turnpike Cars at an outdoor location.

The Dancing Pavilion was highly profitable during the Big Band Era but became the center of a segregation controversy during the 1946 and 1947 seasons. To circumvent the issue, it was turned into a private dance club.

By the late 1930s, the crowds began returning, and prosperity was once again in sight. Ticket sales for 1945 were the highest since 1920. Unfortunately, after 1945 the park never again reported such high ticket sales. During the war years the park faced shortages of both manpower and materials. New rides were simply not available, and most maintenance supplies were in short supply. The park's souvenir stand sold 43,000 balloons in 1937. By 1942, however, rubber was needed for the war effort, and balloons were not sold again until the 1948 season. Still, industry was working around the clock and war-weary families needed recreation and an excuse to divert thoughts from the war. Some parks, like Akron's Summit Beach, even tried 24-hour operations in order to accommodate the schedules of plant workers.

During the 1950s, Euclid Beach made an effort to modernize Kiddieland in the Colonnade. One new addition was the Helicopter ride, which permitted young riders to raise and lower their helicopter by moving the lap bar forward or pulling it back.

Euclid Beach purchased its first Dodgem cars in 1921, but in 1930 the Humphreys bought sixty "modern" cars from the Dodgem Corporation of Lawrence, Massachusetts. With the new complement of cars, Euclid Beach claimed to have the largest Dodgem installation in the United States.

In spite of the difficulties of operating an amusement park during wartime, Euclid Beach thrived. With the rationing of gasoline and tires, a streetcar line that made the park accessible to virtually every Cleveland resident gave Euclid Beach a decided advantage. The Big Band Era, in full swing during the war years, also contributed to a series of successful seasons. Although there was a time when military uniforms were prohibited in the Dance Pavilion, service personnel on leave were a daily fixture from 1942 to 1945. The ballroom's long-standing segregation policy, however, was maintained and African-Americans had no hope of dancing at Euclid Beach.

Soon after the war ticket sales at Euclid Beach began a long and painful descent that continued throughout the fifties. The booming postwar birth rate certainly benefited the park, but the true golden age of the amusement park industry was unquestionably over. Men who flew real fighter aircraft in combat were only marginally entertained by amusement rides that simulated flight. Furthermore, increasing numbers of automobiles gave Americans a newfound mobility, and

In 1948, Euclid Beach replaced the old compressed air–driven steam engine with the new, streamlined "Euclid Beach Chief." The Model G-16 train from the Miniature Train Company remained in service until the park's final season.

The Mill Chute, the park's first aquatic ride, appeared for the 1921 season. In 1937, the Mill Chute was redesigned, rebuilt, and renamed Over the Falls. Its 50-degree drop made it steeper than any of the park's coasters.

Euclid Beach had operated a Ferris wheel in 1896, but it was almost seventy years before another wheel was installed. A Big Eli wheel, purchased in 1966 and placed where the Great American Racing Derby once stood, was the last new major ride added at the Beach.

Held securely in place by a ladder, young visitors to the Colonnade could enjoy a ride on the park's Kiddie Hook & Ladder fire truck. Although the Hook & Ladder moved slowly around a concrete course, a bell and a siren provided some excitement.

the annual family vacation contributed to the declining popularity of amusement parks. The tragic polio epidemic during these years gave thousands of parents a reason to fear crowds; and many of them kept their children safely at home in front of the family TV.

Given their tenacious spirit it's no surprise that the Humphrey Company continued to fight for increased patronage by making even more improvements to the park. From 1949 to 1957 they entertained baby boomers with annual additions of new kiddie rides. Euclid Beach was one of the few amusement parks to protect young children from both sun and rain by placing the kiddie rides in the shelter of the Colonnade.

In 1959, Dudley S. Humphrey III took over park management when his father, Harvey, died. Under Dudley's direction, major rides were added, among them the Turnpike and the Antique Autos, installed in the Skating Rink in 1963 after roller-skating was suspended. The park's last significant ride additions, a Big Eli Ferris wheel and a Tilt-A-Whirl, were purchased in 1966.

Throughout the amusement industry, declining attendance was forcing the closure of once-popular facilities. Many local parks, including Puritas Springs Park, Akron's Summit Beach Park, and Vermilion's Crystal Beach Park, finally gave up and padlocked their gates.

☞

Although the Aero Dips was the park's oldest and least exciting coaster, it remained popular. The Aero Dips was the wise choice for those who did not dare to sample the wild Flying Turns or the Thriller (pictured below).

At the time the Allan Herschell Company introduced the Hurricane ride, Euclid Beach was in the market for some new rides to expand the midway. In 1949, the park paid $29,567.01 to be one of the first parks to operate a Hurricane.

Still Euclid Beach held on tightly even as other parks around it closed. Ticket sales never again reached the incredible 19,989,057 sold in 1945, but nevertheless, the fifties were profitable for the Humphrey Company. Inevitably, though, declining attendance took its toll on Euclid Beach. By 1965, ticket booth sales were down to 11,356,919. Three years later Dudley Humphrey confessed, "Our expenses are outrunning our income. It has been that way for the past five seasons." All hope for business recovery was lost. Furthermore, just an hour and a half to

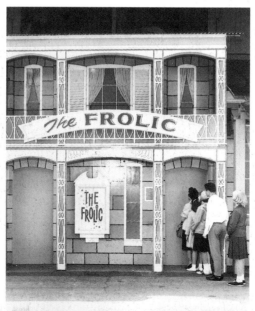

☜

The Swinging Gym ride (called Flying Cages in most parks) was added 1964. The Giant Slide had been built three years earlier. Neither ride proved very popular, and both were sold at the end of the 1966 season.

The Frolic, more of an illusion than a ride, enjoyed a very short tenure at Euclid Beach. Part of the early 1960s modernization efforts, it was sold and removed in 1965.

the west, Cedar Point was emerging as a superpark. Euclid Beach could not hope to compete, and the Humphrey Company entered into an option agreement with developer Dominic Visconsi. In June of 1968, Visconsi publicly announced that "Euclid Beach Park has only two more seasons to go." While Visconsi made plans to convert the old park into high-rise residential housing, Euclid Beach limped sadly through her two final seasons. The park finally closed forever on September 28, 1969. Like the grand lady she had always been, Euclid Beach was impeccably maintained and operated to the very end.

After the park closed, some rides were moved to Streetsboro, where the Humphreys opened Shady Lake Park (1978–1982). The Bug cars were sold to Geauga Lake Park, and the carousel traveled to Old Orchard Beach, Maine. All of the

With the trees bare and snow on the ground, the buildings, rides, and boundaries of Euclid Beach are clearly visible. The large open area was the main parking lot.

roller coasters, the Over the Falls ride, and many buildings were razed. Several of the larger buildings, including the 1895 Dance Pavilion, were destroyed at the hands of arsonists. After Shady Lake Park was closed, the Humphrey Company continued to manufacture their famous popcorn, popcorn balls, and candy kisses—tasty reminders of cherished times spent at Euclid Beach Park, one of America's greatest amusement parks.

After the Big Band Era came to an end, the Dance Pavilion stood quiet and empty much of the time. The area in the foreground served briefly as an outdoor dance area during the 1920s.

I REMEMBER . . . Saturday, September 29, 1951 . . . Back at Public Square, I bought a newspaper and there was a big ad for Euclid Beach Park . . . it was the last weekend of the season and all rides would be 5 cents. So, we boarded a PCC car on Superior Avenue. No longer did they run to Euclid Beach Park, so we had to get a Route 44 bus to get to Euclid Beach Park. It was a very chilly evening, about 40 degrees, and I had on a leather jacket as we rode most all of the rides, including, of course, the Thriller, Racing Coaster, Flying Turns, and Over the Falls. We had a great time.

Last visit to Euclid Beach Park was in August 1969, but I did visit there several times in the 1960s. I was very impressed with the park as they had three band organs. The huge orchestrion played for the skaters. Of course the merry-go-round had a band organ, but the one I liked was the little one at the base of the Rocket ride that you could listen to while waiting to ride the Rocket Ships.— *Richard L. Bowker*

As Euclid Beach started losing money, the Humphreys were forced to reduce maintenance costs. The pier, which produced no revenues, was allowed to fall into disrepair, and during the final season much of the structure had already collapsed into the lake.

Luna Park

Luna Park, like most other parks, was successful because of excellent streetcar service from anywhere in the city. This Cleveland streetcar, stopped at East 110th Street and Woodland Avenue, carried a Luna crescent moon sign in the right front window, indicating that it stopped at the park.

*N*ineteen hundred and three was a watershed year in the development and history of the amusement park industry. A year earlier, Fred Thompson and Elmer "Skip" Dundy purchased Paul Boyton's Sea Lion Park (1895–1902) at New York's Coney Island. During the winter, they razed everything except Boyton's Shoot-the-Chutes ride and constructed an entirely new installation based on Thompson's detailed ideas and plans. Even though he was frequently inebriated, the brilliant Thompson created the world's most spectacular amusement facility and named it Luna Park. Architecturally unique, the delightful Luna featured an unorthodox blend of Arabic, Teutonic, Chinese, Japanese, French, Moorish, and Byzantine styles. Historian John Kasson has described it as "Super-Saracen or Oriental Orgasmic" architecture. The gaudy designs were topped with towers, domes, and minarets, giving the park a dynamic verticality. At dusk, 250,000 incandescent bulbs turned Thompson's "designed confusion" into a visually sensual fairyland.

Luna Park opened to a crowd of 45,000 amazed visitors on May 16, 1903. The park immediately won the hearts of New Yorkers and the attention of amusement industry entrepreneurs. Among those who viewed the new park with interest was Frederick Ingersoll of Pittsburgh. One of the most influential men in the early amusement park arena, Ingersoll owned the Ingersoll Engineering & Construction Company. By 1904, his firm had built twenty-three roller coasters, four Old Mill rides, and thirty-six fun houses. Ingersoll then turned his attention to constructing entire parks based upon Thompson's Luna Park model. In 1905, he opened two new Luna Parks, one in Cleveland and one in Pittsburgh.

Ingersoll traveled to Cleveland in 1904, raised $300,000 through investors, and incorporated the Ingersoll Amusement Company. He then carefully selected a 31-acre site located at the northeastern corner of Woodhill Road and Woodland Avenue. The park's future home was situated on a major Cleveland streetcar line, making it accessible to virtually all Clevelanders.

During the winter of 1904–05, five hundred carpenters and one hundred electricians, plumbers, and painters rushed to complete the park in time for a spring opening. Thanks to a carefully planned publicity blitz, public anticipation ran high. Finally, on May 18, 1905, the gates to Luna Park swung open. On May 21, the first Sunday of operations, the streetcar lines strained to carry fifty thousand people to visit the spectacular new park.

The neat, orderly appearance of the midway was a hallmark of all of Fred Ingersoll's Luna Parks throughout the country. In this early view, probably 1905, the park's concert stage spans the Shoot-the-Chutes hill. Later, the stage was moved to another location.

At the very center of Luna Park was the Shoot-the-Chutes ride. Designed by global adventurer and park owner Paul Boyton, the ride had been the focal point of Luna Park when it opened at Coney Island in 1903. Thereafter, it was difficult to construct a Luna Park without a Shoot-the-Chutes and its large lagoon at the epicenter of the park.

If visitors found themselves gawking at the profusion of color and architectural styles, they were equally amazed by the entertainments offered by Cleveland's new Luna Park. Among the one hundred features and attractions were such headline attractions as Shoot-the-Chutes, Scenic River, Shooting the Shoe (giant slide), Electric Theatre, Chateau Alphonse (fun house), a Figure Eight roller coaster, and a Trip to Rockaway (simulated ship cruise). The fact that Luna would not be operating in the same conservative vein as Euclid Beach was evidenced by the Japanese Exposition, which advertised "Pretty Geisha Girls in Native Costumes." Like Coney Island's Luna, the Cleveland park provided a nonstop bill of entertainment. During the first few weeks of operations, Luna presented Ingersoll's Red Cockade Band, troupes of Japanese and Russian acrobats and dancers, an outdoor circus, and Gertrude Breton, a daring lady who leaped a chasm in an automobile. The park engaged a number of local concert bands including those of Ciricillo, Gugliotta, and Frank Russo. Russo, composer of the "Cedar Point March," bestowed the same honor on Luna with the "Luna Park

I REMEMBER . . . I went to Euclid Beach for seventy years, and we always loved the Beach. But Luna Park was special. We took the streetcars to the park. Luna Park was beautiful. It had so many colored lights. When you were old enough to date, you always hoped your date would take you to Luna. Euclid Beach was more for the kids and families. The dance hall was the most beautiful in Cleveland. In 1941 I saw Luna Park at Coney Island. Our Luna was even better. — *Jessie Hammerstrom*

March." Management also signed contracts with some of the nation's major touring bands; such renowned units as John Duss's New York Band, Don Phillippini's Band, Fraser's Highlander Band, and Alessandro Liberati's Military Band and Grand Opera Company all entertained at Cleveland's Luna Park.

Meanwhile, the Humphreys at Euclid Beach also employed concert bands but certainly did not approve of many of Luna's more common offerings. Beer flowed

The new ballroom (at left), seen from the top of the Shoot-the-Chutes ride, occupied a commanding position on the main midway. By this time, the shore of the lagoon was lined with game and food stands and a popular barbecued roast beef counter. On the right are the Belfry for Bats fun house and the Rifle Range.

In addition to famous national concert bands, Luna Park presented the best of the local Cleveland bands. Among the most popular was the Ciricillo Concert Band directed by Salvatore Ciricillo. The white-uniformed and mustachioed bandleader posed with his musicians at the park's entrance around 1910.

The nattily attired Casa Nova Orchestra was one of the many bands that performed in Luna's redecorated ballroom during the dance-crazy 1920s. Even local bands like those of Austin Wylie and Emerson Gill brought thousands out to dance. On an average Sunday, Luna sold 15,000 dance tickets, and even for Thursday evenings ticket sales of 7,000 were recorded.

The Casa Nova Orchestra

Chateau Alfonse was a fun house, identical to one by the same name that Fred Ingersoll operated at Cedar Point. The Old Shoe was one of the most interesting and imaginative slides ever constructed. It was, like most rides of the early 1900s, built for adult use and designed to show as much female leg as the law would allow.

When Luna's original ballroom opened in 1905, it was the most elaborate dancing pavilion ever seen in the Cleveland area. The park's management had misjudged the popularity of dancing at Luna, and within a few years, it was recognized that the ballroom was far too small to accommodate the huge crowds.

freely at Luna as management strove to cater to the tastes of European immigrants and their descendants, who prized the beverage as part of their heritage. While the sale of beer did not concern the Catholic Mutual Benevolent Association, which brought twenty thousand people to the park, it did offend the Cleveland Christian Endeavor, scheduled for an outing on August 19, 1905. When the officers of the CCE learned of Luna's beer garden they promptly moved the event to alcohol-free Euclid Beach. For most patrons, however, the chance to cool off with a cold beer was simply an added incentive to visit what became, prior to 1918, Cleveland's favorite amusement park.

Other Luna attractions would also have been spurned by Euclid Beach. In 1906 Dr. F. H. Schenheim charged admission to his exhibit of live human premature babies in incubators. Even though the exhibit utilized trained doctors and nurses and the babies were kept in state-of-the-art incubators, some felt the exhibit exploited the babies in what was basically a sideshow.

By the 1920s, Luna Park was being modernized with new rides and attractions. In this view, taken from the new Pippin roller coaster, a Dodgem building has been constructed and the Shoot-the-Chutes lagoon has been converted into Monkey Island.

The Mystic River (originally named the Scenic River in 1905) was a very popular ride, especially with romantic young couples. Except for illuminated scenes, the ride's canals were dark and quiet. Officially, Luna frowned on public displays of affection, but "unintentional" contact in the Mystic River, on roller coasters, and in the fun houses was beyond the park's control

Many of Luna's entertainments were either highly suggestive or blatantly sexual in nature. DeKreke's Mysterious Asia show had been a big hit at the 1904 World's Fair and came to Luna with a company of performers that included native dancing girls in exotic and revealing costumes. The Burlesque Bull Fight and Spanish Ballet, Trostler's "In Cupid's Garden," and the Broadway Beauty Chorus attracted paying customers by presenting lines of shapely ladies in as little clothing as was legally acceptable. The Creation show, direct from the London Palace, opened with a group of attractive ladies posed as statuary. On cue they evolved into living, dancing girls whirling about the stage in seductive costumes. Throughout its career, Luna raised the ire of the city's clergymen. Both Protestant ministers and Catholic priests branded Luna a "School of Vice." Elwood Salsbury, the park's publicity director and later general manager, insisted that Luna's shows were de-

In its heyday, even a rainy day did not dampen the spirits of the happy crowds at Luna Park. Signs in foreground (right) promise that, the Scenic Railway is the most "thrilling ride of the century." In the background a banner announces "Six American Girls," a show that revealed the sexual undertones at Luna and many other parks.

Every time the newspapers published another "Luna Park scandal," more and more men stood in long lines to purchase tickets for the salacious presentations.

Albert Chatfield, standing with the ballroom behind him, owned a Cleveland photographic studio and ran the park's souvenir photo gallery. Thousands commemorated their visit to Luna with a photo from Bert's gallery. After Luna closed in 1929, Chatfield moved his summer studio to Chippewa Lake Park.

I REMEMBER . . . My uncle was Bert Chatfield. He was a photographer in Cleveland and ran the photo studio at Luna Park during the summer. Our whole family would go out to visit Uncle Bert, and he always had tickets for us. Maybe because Uncle Bert was there, it was our favorite park.

I have always loved horses, so I rode the merry-go-round every chance I got. When Uncle Bert moved his photo studio to Chippewa Lake Park around 1930 he got me a job at Chippewa. I lived with my aunt and uncle in "Chat-a-While" cottage, and along with doing other jobs, I ran the merry-go-round. — *Walter S. Francis*

cent and simply portrayed ethnic dancers just as they would appear in the "old country." In any case, every time the newspapers published another "Luna Park scandal," more and more men stood in long lines to purchase tickets for the salacious presentations.

Taking advantage of the so-called "bad" publicity generated by Luna's alcohol sales and sexual innuendo, park management moved blissfully ahead, adding new rides, attractions, and shows. Because of the phenomenal public interest in aviation, Luna brought three important early aviators to Cleveland. A. Roy Kna-

Luna's management, always attuned to public tastes, was quick to make aviation part of the park's attraction fare. In 1906, "Airship Week" featured two of America's best-known and most daring aeronauts, Lincoln Beachey and A. Roy Knabenshue, in dirigible exhibition flights over the park. Balloons, parachute drops, and fixed-wing aircraft also made appearances at Luna.

benshue, Frank Goodale, and Lincoln Beachey made daily flights over the park in their dirigibles. German aeronaut Adolph Wullman ascended toward the sky in his "War Balloon," and J. O. Gill thrilled spectators by parachuting to earth from a balloon. Attempting to beat Glenn Curtiss on a planned flight to Cedar Point in 1910, C. W. Cain tried to launch a fixed-wing aircraft from Luna, but the plane was destroyed when it struck one of Luna's fences.

Luna's popularity is evident in this excerpt from a June 1906 letter sent by one Clevelander to a friend: "Visited fair Luna on Saturday evening for the second

Free acts were a major attraction and, as this photo suggests, drew large crowds. In 1913, Max "Dare Devil" Schreyer rode a bicycle down a 142-foot ramp, launched himself high in the air, and landed in a small pool. He performed this act 2,020 times, but was killed in 1919 while making his 2,021st attempt at Van Cortlandt Park in New York.

Cleveland businessman and politician Matthew F. Bramley was an original 1905 investor in the company that built and operated Luna Park. In 1911, when Ingersoll was in deep financial difficulties, Bramley obtained control of the park and formed the Luna Park Amusement Company. Under Bramely's direction, Luna Park was expanded and modernized.

By the 1920s, the automobile was replacing the streetcar as the vehicle of choice for the journey to Luna Park. While Luna adjusted by building larger parking lots, the auto was a mixed blessing. Now, anyone who owned a family car could bypass Luna and easily travel to Cedar Point, Geauga Lake, Crystal Beach, Chippewa Lake, or a dozen other parks that had previously been less convenient to reach.

time this season. Will go again next Saturday when the Protective Home Circle hold their picnic." Because most Clevelanders shared this affection for the park, Luna prospered. The park's primary shareholder, however, was wallowing in a financial abyss. Frederick Ingersoll was financially overextended. By 1908, the Ingersoll Amusement Company was having difficulty making payments related to the Cleveland park, and a year later Pittsburgh's Luna Park closed its gates forever. In 1910, 133 creditors were bombarding Ingersoll for $179,668.94 in debts. Other shareholders in Cleveland's Luna anticipated Ingersoll's financial demise and formed the Luna Park Amusement Company. The Ingersoll Amusement Company was sold to the new company for a rumored $100,000.

The financial and spiritual leader of the new company was Matthew F. Bramley, an original 1905 Luna investor. Born on a farm in Independence, Ohio, Bramley was the living embodiment of Horatio Alger. After years of laboring at menial jobs, he founded the Trinidad Paving Company, which, in time, became the largest street-paving concern in the world. He later founded the Templar Motors Corporation, became an active Republican politician, and headed several scientific expeditions. Yet, despite his strenuous business schedule, Bramley found time to serve as Luna's manager in 1911. In 1912, however, he hired Colonel Charles X. Zimerman to run the park. A well-known Ohio National Guard officer, Zimerman proved to be an outstanding park manager.

Under the Bramley-Zimerman administration, Luna Park ascended to new heights.

The two men continued to offer the kinds of attractions that had contributed to Luna's success, including airship flights over Cleveland. Captain and Mrs. Jack Dallas were engaged to pilot the dirigible *Luna II*. After that airship was destroyed in a thunderstorm, the company spent $5,000 to build the *Luna III*. Mrs. Dallas was one of the first female airship pilots in the United States; she and Captain Dallas made headlines when they taught Eleanor Jamities, a nineteen-year-old Luna ticket-taker, to fly airships.

By 1912 America was dance crazy, and it seemed that new dances (some not acceptable in "proper" ballrooms) were sweeping the country almost daily. In addition, Vernon and Irene Castle introduced the popular "society dances." In an attempt to eradicate those new dances that were considered immoral, vice commissions and social reformers launched major assaults on dance halls. The ballrooms

In 1917, Bramley allotted $100,000 for the construction of a new ballroom with 18,000 square feet of dance floor. Cleveland was astounded by the size and beauty of the new pavilion, and one newspaper reporter declared, "The floor is perfect, the music—shall we say adorable?" The new structure was equipped with a soda counter to refresh the dancers.

Among the new rides to appear on Luna's midway during the 1920s was the popular new Caterpillar. The invention of a Pennsylvanian, Hyla F. Maynes, the Caterpillar featured a canvas cover that plunged riders into darkness as the ride's speed accelerated. It was a big hit with young couples when centrifugal force threw young ladies into the arms of their escorts.

at Cleveland's amusement parks were operated with decorum, but some of the city's 130 dance halls were not so concerned with propriety. As a result, Cleveland's mayor appointed dance hall inspectors to oversee all ballrooms, including Luna's. Luna maintained a high level of supervision on the dance floor, and it was reported that "Luna Park deserves high praise for the standard which it has set." As dancing became big business, Bramley spent $100,000 in 1917 to build a new ballroom with 18,000 square feet of dance floor. At the time, Luna was the city's leading summer facility for dancing.

By modern roller coaster standards, Luna's Scenic Railway was small, slow, and lacking in thrills. When it opened in 1906, however, it was the largest roller coaster Clevelanders had ever seen.

Just before the 1912 season, Bramley, along with concessionaires Jake Mintz and Charles Salen, took note of a whole new craze: motorcycle racing. The first motordrome, a circular wooden track with steeply banked sides, was built at Playa del Ray, California, in 1910. Observing the instant popularity of the new thrill sport, Bramley, Mintz, and Salen acted quickly. On May 18, 1912, Luna Stadium, the nation's fifth motordrome, with seating for ten thousand spectators, debuted.

In the shadow of a roller coaster, crowds enjoy a concert or sporting event at Luna Stadium. Wooden seats and no protection from the summer sun made it uncomfortable for lengthy events.

Daredevil racers from all over the world drove their cycles at speeds of up to 100 miles per hour along the high sloping wall of Luna's Stadium. The popularity of the dangerous new sport was equaled only by its risks. At Luna, Robert "Daredevil" Hunter lost his life in a race, while eight people were killed in one accident at New Jersey's Electric Park. When it appeared that Cleveland mayor Newton D. Baker might take steps to close Luna's profit-

The train of the Jack Rabbit coaster exhibits the typical design of pre-1920 roller-coaster cars. They were built by the Philadelphia Toboggan Company, a firm that is still a leader in coaster car design and construction.

The Motordrome, probably the first such installation east of the Mississippi River, opened in 1912. The stadium seated ten thousand, and the excitement of motorcycle racing on a banked track drew huge crowds of spectators. However, injuries, deaths, and a great deal of noise doomed the operation. It closed early in the 1914 season and was converted into Luna Stadium and used for pageants and sporting events.

able motordrome, Bramley took action to improve safety and reduce noise. Even so, after two cyclists and three spectators were injured in yet another accident, Bramley suspended motorcycle racing at Luna. On June 17, 1914, Luna Stadium reopened as a bicycle track, arena, and football stadium.

Bramley spared no effort or expense on his beloved amusement park. In 1915, $160,000 was slated for park improvements. A major portion of that budget was earmarked for the Philadelphia Toboggan Company, which had provided Bramley with a plan for an elaborate new carousel as well as a modern, high-speed roller coaster. The proposed Jack Rabbit coaster, designed by Joseph McKee, was probably an attempt to keep pace with Euclid Beach, where the Derby Racer opened in 1913. In time, Luna's midway was amplified with a 123-foot Ferris wheel from Walter P. Shaw, a Mangels Whip, the Cave of the Winds, and two fun houses, Hilarity Hall and the Belfrey for Bats.

During this time Luna was perched at the zenith of its popularity as Cleveland's favorite amusement park. In 1916 Luna hosted 1,967,435 visitors, and the follow-

ing season brought even larger crowds. Concessionaires reported their revenues had soared by 25 percent. On the surface, Luna's future seemed as secure as its past, but the seeds of her decline were already planted. Park manager Zimerman left with the 5th Infantry for Mexican Border service in 1916, and in 1917 the soon-to-be general was in France with the 37th Division. For six long years Luna struggled along without the direction of her highly competent manager as he served in the military. Even more devastating to the park, however, was Prohibition, which went into effect on July 1, 1919. Luna's prosperity had floated along on the sale of beer since 1905. Now that the sale of beer was illegal, Luna faced the loss of huge revenues. Furthermore, without the sale of beer, Luna would have a difficult time competing with the rapidly expanding Euclid Beach. Attendance figures tell the story: in 1919, Luna's attendance fell to 1,000,000 while Euclid Beach entertained

The park's Roller Skating Rink continued to operate long after most of Luna had been razed. Vandals tried unsuccessfully to burn the rink six times. On December 11, 1938, the last vestige of Luna Park was consumed by fire.

I REMEMBER . . . John Miller, the world's greatest coaster builder, hired me as a carpenter in 1919. I traveled all over during the 1920s and built coasters and other rides at all kinds of parks. Miller sent me to Cleveland to build the Pippin at Luna Park. It was a good coaster but nothing special. Just an average Miller coaster and not like the Cyclone at Puritas Springs that H. S. Smith designed for Miller. Most people think Miller designed that one, but he was too busy and Smith helped with designs. Luna Park was the most beautiful park ever built. I have seen most parks, and there was nothing like it. When the lights were turned on it took your breath away. — *A. M. Brown*

1,250,000. Twenty-five thousand people visited Euclid Beach on an average Sunday, while only 20,000 chose to go to Luna. On a typical Thursday, there were 6,000 people at Luna, but 12,000 at Euclid Beach.

Following the economic recession of 1920–21, new attractions, aggressive advertising, and increased publicity attested to the fact that General Zimerman had returned from military service to once again manage Luna Park. However, in 1926, Zimerman died unexpectedly, and Bramley replaced him with another Ohio National Guard officer, Colonel Clarence F. Bluem.

Colonel Bluem inherited a difficult situation. Over the years, Bramley's dedication to Luna had been redirected toward his Templar Motors Corporation. Bramley was also interested in archaeological expeditions, and when a fossilized mastodon was discovered near Johnstown, Ohio, in 1926, he purchased it for $53,000. Bramley agreed to donate the mastodon to the Cleveland Museum of Natural History, provided the museum would allow him to exhibit it at Luna Park for two

Now that the sale of beer was illegal, Luna faced the loss of huge revenues.

seasons. Predictably, few park patrons paid to see the giant fossil, and in early 1928, Colonel Bluem begged the museum to accept the mastodon for its collections immediately.

Luna did expand during the 1920s, but mostly because of the investments of concessionaires, not Bramley. In 1922, Robert B. Loehr and his partners signed a contract with the Luna Park Amusement Company to install and operate rides at the park. The new Pippin Coaster Company hired coaster designer John A. Miller

and paid him $150,000 to construct the Pippin coaster near the park's entrance gate. In subsequent years, Loehr installed the Caterpillar, Tumble Bug, and other rides.

Even with these improvements, by 1927, it was clear that all was not well at Luna. Throughout the country parks were experiencing declines in both attendance and income. Cleveland's short-lived Gordon Gardens failed and was sold to the city in 1927. In Pennsylvania, Conneaut Lake Park was placed in the hands of a receiver. And, at Cedar Point, President George A. Boeckling predicted economic catastrophe and curtailed expansion.

Luna faced the same decline in income as many other parks, and in July 1927 Bramley stopped making weekly payments to the park's concessionaires. At the

After Luna Park abruptly closed at the end of the 1929 season, attempts to reopen the park failed and demolition began. In this photo, taken in 1930, the foundation of the June Bug ride remains in front of the main entrance. In the background is the Pippin roller coaster.

I REMEMBER . . . My mother took me and my brother Bill on the streetcar to Luna Park many times. We also went to Cedar Point, Euclid Beach, and Chippewa Lake. I remember sitting on the bridge that crossed the Shoot-the-Chutes and eating the warm, soft waffles that they sold. Those were the best waffles I ever ate.

My aunt and uncle owned a bungalow right across from the park. When I stayed with them overnight we could sit on the porch and look at the lights and listen to the music from the carousel. That was the prettiest carousel anywhere. I was just a teenager when Luna Park closed, but we were all very sad. — *Jessie M. Francis*

end of the 1928 season, the park owed the Pippin Coaster Company $13,500 and was on the debtor list of many companies. Luna did open in 1929, but many checks were returned to the park for insufficient funds. The Guardian Savings & Trust Company filed suit, and the court ordered the appointment of a receiver. Luna did not open in 1930, and a sheriff's sale disposed of much of the park's equipment. Fortunately for Clevelanders, Luna's magnificent carousel was sold to another Cleveland facility, Puritas Springs Park. J. Harold Bramley, son of the park president, bought what remained of the park for just $72, 534. Bramley intended to rebuild and reopen the park, but these plans never materialized. The roller rink burned in 1938, but by this time the Cleveland Metropolitan Housing Authority already owned an option on the former park lands. By 1941, every trace of Cleveland's once bright and shining star was gone. All of the lights, sounds, sights, and smells that composed Luna Park had been replaced by a neatly planned housing project.

By the spring of 1941, every trace of Luna Park had been erased. In its place rose the neat, modern Woodhill Homes project.

Geauga Lake Park

*I*n 1856, the forerunner of the Erie Railroad laid track alongside a small lake in Aurora, Ohio, a town best known for its cheese making. The first structure to be built near the lake had been a log cabin, in 1817. Decades later, in 1872, Sullivan Giles established a picnic area near the lake, and gradually, the area began to attract summer visitors who enjoyed the picnicking, music, and fishing. By this time the lake was known as Picnic Lake, and the train station that welcomed the passenger trains was dubbed Pond Station.

Alexander G. Kent established the area's first actual summer resort in 1887 on the site of what would later become Geauga Lake Park. Kent's facilities included the Kent House, a seventy-five-room "deluxe" hotel that served pleasing cuisine and featured a large ballroom. In addition to Kent's hotel, a number of cottages also offered vacationers summer accommodations.

Kent's resort offered visitors all of the basic amenities and entertainments that could be found at most late-nineteenth-century American resorts. These included a dancing pavilion, roller-skating rink, bowling alleys, photo gallery, steam-powered carousel, campgrounds, and a parade ground for military encampments. The resort's baseball diamond was often used by the Cleveland National League baseball team, which could not play Sunday games in Cleveland due to local blue laws.

☞

In 1972, Geauga Lake's new admission gate greeted the public for the first time. It was part of an improvement program that began in 1969 and has continued ever since.

By 1888, a steamboat towing a barge equipped with a floating dance floor was operating on the lake that was now known as Geauga. Within a few more years, a large steam launch was also plying Geauga Lake's waters. At various times throughout history launches, rowboats, and canoes were available for rent on Geauga Lake.

The growth of the resort industry around Geauga Lake continued at a relatively slow pace until the 1920s. In 1921, a new ballroom was built by the lakeshore. The increasing popularity of the area attracted the interest of William J. Kuhlman. Kuhlman envisioned an amusement park situated along the lakeshore, and during the winter of 1924–25, Geauga Lake Park was constructed.

While the finishing touches were still being made, Geauga Lake Park opened to the public on Saturday, June 20, 1925. The new park offered free admission, parking for five thousand automobiles, a baseball diamond, tennis courts, horseshoe pits, an athletic field, spacious picnic groves, and dancing in the afternoons and evenings. There were also one hundred new rental rowboats, launches to transport visitors from the railroad station, the

The slightly crescent-shaped Skyrocket, an "out and back" coaster, gives riders a very exciting traditional coaster ride. The domed structure on the right was the park's original carousel building.

The centerpiece of Geauga Lake Park when it opened in 1925 was John A. Miller's spectacular Skyrocket roller coaster. A ride on the Skyrocket cost just 20 cents during that first season, and the coaster proved to be the park's most popular attraction. The archway on the left served as the main entrance to the park.

country's largest shooting gallery, assorted midway games, and a wide range of food services. The ride lineup included a $50,000 John A. Miller–designed roller coaster with a built-in archway that served as the park's entrance. Other rides included a carousel, Whip, Dodgem, Aerial Swing, and miniature railroad.

Incomplete on opening day was the park's mammoth swimming pool. When completed in July, the Olympic-size pool rivaled the huge mosaic Crystal Pool at Akron's Summit Beach Park. The Geauga pool was 110 feet wide and 300 feet long and had a maximum depth of 14 feet. Pool manager E. F. Kubu was a popular water polo player who supervised swimming and diving exhibitions at the park. On July 18, 1926, future film star Johnny Weissmuller set one of his sixty-seven world swimming records when he swam the 220-yard freestyle event in the Geauga pool. Weissmuller, best known for his Tarzan roles, took part in the 1924 and 1928 Summer Olympics, winning five gold medals.

Other sports also played a central role in the early history of Geauga Lake Park. Park owner W. J. Kuhlman was a baseball enthusiast and organized a Class AAA park team in 1926. Comprised primarily of players from the 1925 Cleveland Heights Police team, the park team was managed by Phillip C. Grotenrath.

Among the players recruited were former Cleveland Indian Jack Graney and the son of National League hero Dode Paskert.

Boxing was another popular sport at Geauga Lake Park. In 1931, sportswriters from coast to coast descended on Geauga Lake to see William L. "Young" Stribling train for a July 3 matchup with Max Schmeling in nearby Cleveland. Although he lost that fight and never earned a boxing title, Stribling fought 285 bouts with only

ONE COUPON
GEAUGA LAKE PARK
Skee Ball Alley
REDEEMABLE FOR MERCHANDISE
DURING THE SEASON
ONLY AT THE ABOVE STAND
GLOBE TICKET COMPANY—PHILA
122129

Like Euclid Beach, Geauga Lake offered customers two sizes of Skee Ball alleys. The shorter alleys, built by Wurlitzer, were much easier for children to master. The signs on the posts reminded patrons that spitting spread diseases and was not permitted in the Arcade.

twelve losses. Soon after defeating Maxie Rosenbloom, Stribling was killed in a motorcycle accident.

Geauga Lake Park was also linked indirectly to horse racing. On land adjacent to park property, John A. King and Homer J. Kline constructed the Bainbridge Park race track in 1927. Partially financed by Geauga Lake businessmen, the race track's proximity to Geauga was probably a boon for the amusement park's business.

Beginning with its first day of operation in 1925, Bill Kuhlman found Geauga Lake Park to be a very successful venture. Every Sunday and on holidays, the Erie Railroad ran passenger excursions to the park from the Erie Station at the High Level Bridge. The trains left Cleveland at 10 A.M., picked up passengers at East

The Aeroplane Swing ride (upper right), opened in 1925 and remained popular for more than fifty years. The souvenir stand nearby sold pennants, umbrellas, beach balls, canes, and a variety of other items.

The big Arcade building housed a Dodgem ride on one side and arcade machines, games of chance, and Skee Ball alleys on the other. To the left were three small refreshment stands and the carousel buildings.

I REMEMBER . . . Geauga Lake has its memories. I remember going there in the 1940s, thinking it wasn't much better than going to the local church carnival. Like the church carnival, the midway was filled with games of chance.

One of my daughter Valerie's favorite items is a photo picture pin of her with her grandfather that was made at a midway stand in the late 1960s.

Far from having as many rides as Euclid Beach, the park did have the Rocket Ships and a great carousel.

Probably my favorite place was the Penny Arcade. Besides the exhibit card and other games, I remember one attraction in there that really fascinated me. They had a wishing well type of a structure that you leaned over and looked down into it. Supposedly, what you saw was a mermaid! I was too young to remember to tell you exactly what it looked like other than to tell you I still remember being fascinated by it almost sixty years later.

Sometimes we would also go on the Fourth of July to watch the fireworks show that the park would put on.

The trip to Geauga Lake, unlike the Euclid Beach trip, which took us through the city, took us through rural farm country. I remember reading the Burma Shave signs and also remember the motorcycle policeman hiding behind a billboard on the left side of Aurora Road as we went to the park. I would imagine he caught himself many a speeder on their way to or from the park. — *John F. Szuch*

55th Street and East 93rd Street, and delivered them to Geauga Lake, where they boarded launches for the trip from the train station to the park docks.

Return trains left the park promptly at 8 P.M. Patrons of the park could also take buses that would deposit passengers conveniently at the main entrance. Geauga Lake customers of the 1920s were treated to many amusements, both

☞ The original ballroom, which was later destroyed in a fire, offered dancing every evening except Sundays and on some afternoons. An illuminated sign to the left of the band indicated the type of dance music being played at the time— waltz, one step, fox-trot, Cuban waltz, or others.

For 10 cents the Auto Speedway offered children a chance to drive miniature, battery-powered cars around an oval track. These appear to be Custer Cars, produced by the Custer Specialty Company of Dayton.

exciting and serene. In addition to the Shooting Sky Rocket roller coaster, there were sensational new rides like the Hey Dey and William Mangels's Whip. For the children, Kuhlman installed a miniature aerial swing, miniature railroad, Custer Cars (spelled Kuster Kars at Geauga), a pony track, and a variety of playground equipment. Those who didn't pack a picnic lunch patronized a wide variety of food stands, and J. H. Allendorf offered his famous steaks, chops, and chicken dinners in the cafeteria and restaurant.

Although the park's first five years were prosperous, the faltering economy of the early 1930s brought many concerns for Kuhlman. Nevertheless, he took advantage of declining real estate prices to expand Geauga by purchasing twenty-

Although food was available throughout the park during the 1920s, those seeking a quiet, sit-down dinner walked over to J. H. Allendorf's popular restaurant, situated at the edge of the park along Route 43. Allendorf served seafood and other items, but was best known for his steak and chicken dinners.

Geauga Lake's Olympic-size swimming pool was not ready for opening day but did welcome its first swimmers in July of 1925. It was 110 feet wide by 300 feet long, with a wading pool at one end for children.

two parcels of land totaling 400 acres. As park attendance and spending spiraled downward during the Great Depression, Kuhlman tried out new attractions and promotions in an effort to woo customers. Lavish firework displays depicting "The Battle of Lake Erie" and "The Sinking of the *Lusitania*" were presented on the lake, and Kuhlman worked tirelessly to attract group picnics like those from Garretsville High School, the Cleveland-Sandusky Brewing Company, and any other manufacturing companies and labor unions that could still afford a summer outing. Although little money was available to purchase new rides, Kuhlman spent $35,000 in 1937 to acquire a magnificent eleven-year-old carousel built by the Coney Island master Marcus C. Illions. A prime example of Illions's work, the venerable ride remains a centerpiece at the park.

☞

Hopefully not on duty, a pool life guard joins in the antics on the diving boards. At times, diving acts and competitions were held at the pool, as were swimming races.

In 1934, the park constructed an open-air theater and engaged Handel Wadsworth to stage nightly operas for a fourteen-week run. With a chorus of sixty and a twenty-member ballet troupe, Wadsworth presented a number of popular opera titles, including *The Mikado, The Bohemian Girl, Robin Hood, Sweethearts, The Prince of Pilsen*, and *Said Pasha*. Among the principal performers in the premiere of *The Chimes of Normandy* was Cecile Meinhardt of Akron. But as George Boeckling had discovered years earlier at Cedar Point in Sandusky, most people did not look for highbrow entertainment at amusement parks. Predictably, Wadsworth's operas were not especially successful at Geauga Lake Park.

More successful was the park's ballroom, which threw its doors open to welcome crowds drawn by the Big-Band explosion. Beginning in 1937, many famous big bands swept through Ohio playing the ballrooms at Euclid Beach, Chippewa

Unlike Euclid Beach, Geauga Lake thrived on games of chance and always seemed to have more games than the size of the park justified. At the Ring Toss, players paid 10 cents for three rings and the chance to win prizes by "ringing" one, two, or three wooden ducks.

Geauga Lake's fun house included a giant slide and a series of mechanical devices. For just a 20-cent admission price, visitors could spend as much time as they wished in the fun house. By the 1960s, it was one of the last traditional fun houses surviving in Ohio.

☞

After Prohibition ended, the Geauga Lake Park Company obtained a license to sell alcoholic beverages and opened the Tavern. The Tavern was later converted into a restaurant.

In most parks, the Dodgem was one of the most popular rides—often second only to the roller coaster. Geauga Lake was no exception, and "modern" cars were purchased to update the Dodgem ride that originally opened in 1925.

Lake, Crystal Beach, Summit Beach, Ruggles Beach, and, of course, Geauga Lake. Among these were such greats as Henry Busse and Shep Fields and His Rippling Rhythm. Unlike some other parks, the Geauga Lake ballroom also hosted a number of country-and-western performers, including the Corn Creek Girl's Band and Slim Miller & the Cornhuskers.

Geauga Lake managed to survive the Great Depression, but a decade of poor business had left her rides and buildings looking shabby. The park's dire financial straits were not helped by a severe windstorm that slammed into the park in 1941. The facility sustained $50,000 in damage when trees were felled, buildings were leveled, and a portion of the roller coaster was toppled.

Although there were shortages of labor, maintenance materials, and some foods, prosperity returned during World War II, as companies sought recreational outlets for their overworked employees. At that point, Geauga Lake offered thirty-six rides and a wide variety of games and foods. U-Drive-Em boats, powered by gasoline engines, were added, and the lake was stocked with twenty thousand bluegill and thirty thousand bass to appease a loyal legion of local fishermen.

Kuhlman was again showing a profit with his park when he was killed in an automobile accident in 1945. After his death, Geauga Lake Park was sold to local businessmen Carl Adrian, Harvey Schryer, and Charles Schryer.

While the new owners strove to improve and expand the park, they were beset by their own series of problems. In 1947, the old bath-house was destroyed in an early-season fire

Geauga Lake Park entertained numerous church and school picnics. Supervising schoolchildren, however, did not prevent these nuns from enjoying one of the more tranquil rides.

After World War II, "wet boat" rides became a standard in every park's kiddieland. One of the boats was equipped with an electric motor to drive the ride at a slow speed.

When the roller coaster was renamed, it also received a station facelift that gave it a contemporary look. In the foreground is one of the new ticket booths that also helped give the midway a new appearance.

The 1920s biplane cars on the Aeroplane ride were hopelessly outdated by the late 1930s. To make the ride more appealing, new stainless-steel rocket cars were acquired from the R. E. Chambers Company, and the ride was renamed the Rockets.

that almost spread to the roller coaster and fun house. Later that season, the park was sued for $75,000 when a Cleveland boy suffered some paralysis after an injury on the Dodgem ride. Then, just before the 1952 season, a $500,000 fire incinerated the ballroom, bowling alleys, roller-skating rink, and theater. Once again the roller coaster faced destruction, but was saved by the Aurora Township Fire Department. Finally, in 1954, the park's night watchman was severely wounded when safe crackers unsuccessfully attempted to steal $20,000 from the park's safe.

Despite these setbacks, the park's new owners made progress. During the first eight years of their ownership, they invested $500,000 in the park, eliminated most of the company's old indebtedness, and created an amusement center valued at $1,500,000 (the rides and buildings alone were appraised at $600,000). Company president Charles Schryer designed new kiddie rides as well as new facades for park buildings. A modern bathhouse replaced the one destroyed in the 1947

When first opened, Geauga's rifle range was touted as the largest in the nation. By the time this photo was taken, it had been somewhat reduced in size.

A major portion of the old Recreation Arcade was rebuilt as a cafeteria-style refreshment operation. Giant urns held huge quantities of coffee, a beverage that was in great demand on cooler spring and early fall days.

Not everyone visiting Geauga Lake chose to patronize the park's restaurant or food stands. For those who brought picnic lunches, there was the Picnic Pavilion near the lake. The small refreshment stand sold Vernor's ginger ale, hot coffee, and hot dogs.

fire, and a substantial new dance hall and skating rink cost the company $100,000.

Geauga Lake Park provided jobs for 130 people during the summer months. Although the park operated all of the rides and most of the food stands, a number of concessionaires were granted contracts for other amusements. The roller rink was operated by Dick Dillon and the Arcade by Frank Svoboda. Among those who operated games (and the park had a disproportionate number of games of chance) were Al Grimes, W. J. Winslow, M. G. Wilson, Sid Langman, and Frank Matthews. So popular were the many games that it required $100,000 worth of prizes to meet the demands of customers each season.

During the winter months, a crew of eight men worked to recondition rides and buildings, while Chuck Schryer used that time to book one hundred group picnics for the coming season. Although Geauga Lake Park did not charge admission or maintain turnstiles, Schryer estimated annual attendance at between 1,000,000 and 1,500,000 in 1953.

The quaint miniature electric train continued to operate at Geauga until replaced by a more modern engine and cars after World War II. In the background are two hills of the Skyrocket roller coaster.

By the 1920s, most amusement parks had started to install kiddielands to entertain the children who were still too young for the big midway rides. The Junior Aeroplanes provided a smaller and slower alternative to the large Aeroplane ride enjoyed by older children and adults.

Since the first amusement park opened in 1894, peanuts and popcorn have been midway staples. The smells of roasting peanuts and popping corn made them irresistible to midway passersby.

Another miniaturized version of major ride was the Turtle. A small, gentle model of the Tumble Bug, the Turtle was built by the R. E. Chambers Company in Beaver Falls, Pennsylvania. Despite its diminutive design, it provided plenty of thrills for small children.

Under the experienced direction of the new management team, old Geauga Lake Park was transformed into a modern, well-planned amusement park. One of the first improvements was a monorail that encircled much of the old midway.

With the exception of Cedar Point, which was undergoing a major expansion, most amusement parks were struggling by the mid-1960s. Both Euclid Beach and Chippewa Lake were unable to turn a profit. High labor costs, increasing insurance premiums, and unrelenting maintenance expenses placed the future of Geauga Lake and scores of other traditional parks in question.

Salvation came for Geauga Lake Park in 1968 when four former Cedar Point executives purchased the park and the land for $1,750,000. The new company, Funtime, Inc., was headed by Earl Gascoigne, Gaspar Lococo, Dale Van Voorhis, and Milford Jacobson. They immediately began making improvements for the 1969 season, including a $500,000 monorail system, a new fifteen-ride kiddieland, and a 52-foot-high Ferris wheel.

In 1970, Sea World, which operated a successful marine park in San Diego, California, opened Sea World of Ohio across the lake from Geauga Lake Park.

By the 1950s, the park owners decided to replace the 1925 roller coaster trains with new, streamlined metal cars. At the same time, the Skyrocket was renamed the Clipper.

Although relations between the two parks were sometimes strained, they generally complemented each other and together made Aurora, Ohio, a major tourist destination. That same year, Geauga Lake added several rides including the Himalaya, Tilt-A-Whirl, Flying Coaster, Spider, and Trabant. Gross revenues climbed by 65 percent. Over the next few years, investments in park improvements totaled millions of dollars. New rides, a new admissions gate, and a new park area complete with Western Reserve architecture were all part of a master plan to convert Geauga Lake into one of the nation's better parks.

The Wild Mouse, a steel-tracked roller coaster invented by Ben Schiff, was one of the last additions to old Geauga Lake. The new owners operated it briefly and then sold it to Chippewa Lake Park.

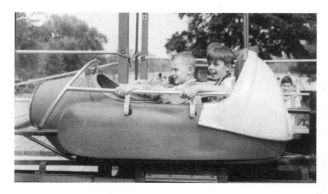

Giant slides, with fiberglass chutes, were popular additions to many amusement park midways during the 1960s and 1970s. Geauga Lake, like Cedar Point, made slides a central attraction.

Capitalizing on the lake, the park's new owners installed an attractive boat ride based on Ohio's historic canal network.

Geauga Dog, the park's famous mascot, was introduced by park sales manager Ron Adams in 1975. It seemed that each year the midway was expanded with new rides and attractions. The water park area was opened in 1983, and five years later the massive Raging Wolf Bobs coaster made its appearance. The new wooden coaster featured an 80-foot first hill and 3,246 feet of track. Ten years later the Texas Twister was installed at a cost of $2,100,000.

Premier Parks, Inc., an Oklahoma City–based operator of amusement and theme parks, purchased Geauga Lake Park from Funtime, Inc., in the mid-1990s. The following year Premier Parks (later known as Six Flags) spent $9 million on improvements at Geauga Lake Park.

When the 2000 season opened, the park's name was changed to Six Flags Ohio, and the parent company spent $40 million to install four roller coasters and make other impressive improvements. In 2001, Six Flags purchased Sea World of Ohio, located just across the lake, and the two operations were combined to form Six Flags Worlds of Adventure.

The new operation was an innovative concept and

certainly made the complex a valuable property. Still, competition from Cedar Point to the west and Kennywood Park in Pittsburgh made life difficult for the Aurora park. Anxious to divest itself of some properties, Six Flags began searching for a buyer after the 2003 season. In early 2004 it was announced that Cedar Fair, parent company of Cedar Point and other major parks, had acquired Six Flags Worlds of Adventure for $145 million.

Once again the park would be locally operated. In short order, it was rechristened Geauga Lake Park, to the delight of thousands of longtime patrons. It remains to be seen what other changes will take place at the park, but for now, it's good to know that the grand old lady of Aurora, Ohio, is still graciously entertaining the public, as she has for the past 130 years.

Although the paint on the facade of the old fun house was looking shopworn, the primitive attraction remained popular until razed to make way for park expansion.

Unlike its predecessors, the new Geauga Lake Park management spent large sums of money to uniform every park employee. The new admission gates announced to every visitor that there were new and exciting attractions beyond the turnstiles.

Because of constant maintenance and loving care, Geauga's classic 1925 roller coaster has survived into the twenty-first century. While small when compared to modern coaster designs, this historic ride still gives riders a maximum of thrills and jolts.

No Intoxicating Beverages or
Persons under the influence
permitted in this Park

ADULTS - 50¢
CHILDREN - 25¢

Puritas Springs Park

*I*t was 1894 when a group of enterprising businessmen began bottling and marketing the mineral-laden water of Puritas Springs located in the Rocky River Valley near Cleveland. The growing popularity of the springs began to draw crowds, and in 1898 the 80-acre site became Puritas Springs Park.

At that time, public transportation was crucial to the success of amusement parks, and the majority of parks built between the late 1890s and 1910 were situated along or at the end of city streetcar or interurban electric lines. Puritas Springs Park was no exception. The electric railway line that became the Cleveland & Southwestern Traction Company in 1903 laid a six-mile branch line in 1898. The new extension traveled out Bellaire Road to Linndale, then alongside Puritas Road until it terminated at Puritas Springs Park. By 1903, the "Green Line" served three major amusement parks: Puritas Springs, Chippewa Lake Park in Medina County, and Seccaium Park, located between Galion and Bucyrus. Originally, all three parks depended heavily on the Green Line for customers, but only Seccaium Park was forced to close when the interurban line abandoned service in 1933.

Puritas Springs Park owed its success to one man, John E. Gooding. Like Dudley S. Humphrey II at Euclid Beach, Gooding lived for his park. Gooding was born

☞ In a traditional amusement park, the owner's entire family pitches in and works. In this photo, Florence Gooding, wife of John Gooding's grandson, sells tickets on a busy day.

in Somersetshire, England, in 1864. Four years later his family emigrated and set-tled on a farm near Orwell, Ohio. Around 1890, Gooding entered the amusement industry when he began operating steam-powered carousels at carnivals and fairs. Years later, he sold some of his portable rides to his cousins, Roy, Arby, and Floyd E. Gooding, who developed the Gooding Amusement Company, for many years the largest portable outdoor amusement company in the world. It was apparently one of his steam carousels that John Gooding installed at the new Puritas Springs Park in 1898, and in 1901 he leased the entire park from the electric railway company. Once established as manager, Gooding built a house for his family on the park grounds so that he could keep a constant watch over his park.

By the time the 1911 season rolled around Puritas Springs was still a small, but growing, amusement park. It had just a few rides, including a carousel and a Ferris wheel, but there were also other attractions such as bowling, billiards, a baseball diamond, picnic areas, a range of food offerings, and a campground available ". . . free to desirable parties." That season $30,000 was spent to construct a new dance hall, which opened just before the big July Fourth holiday.

Like many electric railway companies, the Cleveland Southwestern gradually lost interest in owning and operating amusement parks. Accordingly, they sold Puritas Springs Park to Gooding in May of 1915. Now sole owner, Gooding was able to make improvements to his park without the restrictions of a lease.

Gooding spent little money on advertising, and he rarely obtained press coverage. In 1919, however, Puritas Springs Park was at the center of a well-publicized

John E. Gooding was the heart and soul of Puritas Springs Park. Living on the park grounds, he lovingly watched over the park and built it into a major amusement enterprise. After he died from complications of diabetes, his family operated the park for another thirty years.

Like so many other early amusement parks, Puritas Springs Park was a "Trolley Park." It was founded by the Cleveland & Southwestern interurban railway, and the line's cars stopped at the park's rustic gates.

The first major building at Puritas Springs was the Pavilion, which served primarily as the park's ballroom. The Pavilion's architecture was very typical for park buildings of the early 1900s, but the all-wood structure created a serious fire hazard.

The first carousel at Puritas Springs appears to have been an early Herschell Riding Gallery. The ride was probably originally steam powered but was converted to electricity when installed at the park.

racial controversy. Since 1909, Emancipation Day (which celebrated the end of slavery in America) had brought large crowds of African-Americans to Luna Park. Luna, however, was a segregated operation, admitting blacks on only a few selected days. And, on these days, the swimming area was always closed. Such policies were not unusual in the amusement industry, and most American parks were either totally or partially segregated. Chestnut Hill Park in Philadelphia, for example, steadfastly denied admission to nonwhites. In Cleveland, Euclid Beach denied blacks access to the ballroom as early as 1895, and both Luna and Euclid Beach admitted blacks on certain "Jim Crow Days."

The promoters of Emancipation Day came under increasing criticism when each year the pool at Luna was drained of water and declared closed for maintenance on the day of the picnic. Luna's management tolerated rather than welcomed Emancipation Day, and the event committee finally tired of Luna's attitude. With Euclid Beach maintaining its discriminatory policy, the committee turned to Puritas

☞

Springs Park, where Gooding cordially welcomed the event. Emancipation Day of 1919 attracted thousands of African-Americans who traveled from as far away as Youngstown and Sandusky to enjoy baseball games, a beauty contest, a baby show, and a series of field races and other contests. Unfortunately for Puritas Springs Park, the event was discontinued in 1920. When it was reestablished in 1922, the Emancipation Day committee shunned Puritas Springs and returned to Luna.

The decade of the 1920s proved prosperous for Puritas Springs, and Gooding launched a major campaign to expand the park with new rides. He was able to construct new refreshment stands, and he also purchased several major rides, added a footbridge over the ravine, and installed a Magic Carpet fun house. In addition, new games appeared, including Skee Ball alleys. During the winter of 1927–28, he hired legendary

On Cleveland Press Day, a long line of children wait to ride the Tumble Bug. Newspapers treated newsboys to outings at amusement parks each summer and also stimulated readership by giving away free tickets for certain days.

While younger children enjoyed the kiddieland, teenagers favored the close-contact activities of the Roller Skating Rink. Although the rink was sometimes criticized for its segregation policies, the skating floor was often filled to capacity from March to October.

Perhaps one of the most beautiful carousels ever constructed, the Puritas Springs ride began life in 1915 at Cleveland's Luna Park. Those who did not elect to ride a horse were comfortably seated in one of the large Romanesque chariots.

The great carousel at Puritas Springs featured two Roman-style chariots pulled by two majestic, straining steeds.

☞

Located on the main midway were the Fun House (right) and the Ghost Town. The Ghost Town, later named the Pretzel, was a ride-through dark ride built by the Pretzel Amusement Company.

roller coaster builder John A. Miller to construct a ravine coaster that took advantage of the park's rugged geography. Although Augie Miller generally did all the design work on his coasters, he was particularly busy at this time, and it appears that his superintendent, H. S. Smith, did the initial drawings on what would become the Cyclone.

HOUSE
ONE COUPON
Good For Merchandise
PURITAS SPRINGS PARK

Mgr._____
SAVE YOUR COUPON FOR BETTER PRIZES

73

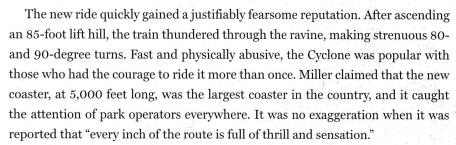

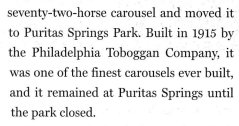

The new ride quickly gained a justifiably fearsome reputation. After ascending an 85-foot lift hill, the train thundered through the ravine, making strenuous 80- and 90-degree turns. Fast and physically abusive, the Cyclone was popular with those who had the courage to ride it more than once. Miller claimed that the new coaster, at 5,000 feet long, was the largest coaster in the country, and it caught the attention of park operators everywhere. It was no exaggeration when it was reported that "every inch of the route is full of thrill and sensation."

After Luna Park closed in 1929, Gooding spent $27,000 to purchase Luna's seventy-two-horse carousel and moved it to Puritas Springs Park. Built in 1915 by the Philadelphia Toboggan Company, it was one of the finest carousels ever built, and it remained at Puritas Springs until the park closed.

Not surprisingly, Puritas Springs Park struggled to survive the Great Depression. Furthermore, the cessation of service by the Cleveland & Southwestern interurban line dealt the park another

After World War II, the aging original Whip ride was replaced with a new, streamlined Whip from Mangels's Coney Island factory. The Whip was always popular with both adults and children.

In 1928, Gooding engaged prolific coaster engineer John A. Miller to build the Cyclone coaster. Designed to utilize the ravines of the park, the Cyclone became a respected and feared coaster. Although only one fatality occurred on the Cyclone, it had a well-deserved reputation for providing a wild and violent ride.

economic blow. As if these problems were not enough, a portion of the dance hall floor collapsed in 1932, dumping a hundred dancers in a heap and sending thirteen to the hospital. The economy had slowly begun to recover by the late 1930s, but then John Gooding died on December 10, 1937. Fortunately, the Gooding family stepped in and continued to operate the park to the high standards established by its founder. Gooding's daughter, Pearl C. Visoky, became president of the Puritas Springs Park Company, and her husband James also took an active role in management until his death in 1940.

☞

Another new addition to the postwar midway was the fast and exciting Moon Rocket ride. The ride and the centerpiece turned in opposite directions, creating the illusion of extreme speed.

I REMEMBER . . . My sister and I grew up about four blocks from the park. We were ten years old in 1958, and we both attended Puritas Elementary School with both the Gooding boys, Jim and John. The best times we had were on their birthdays because we always got invited to their house (on the park grounds) for a party, which included free run of the park and the rides. Mr. and Mrs. Gooding were always very nice to the children, very gracious indeed.

I was a member in good standing of Jungle Larry's Club.

I remember the big fire as the sky turned orange in our backyard and the park burned. — *Marshall Moore*

Within limited budgets, the new operators continued to expand the park. In 1942, a Moon Rocket ride was introduced, and nine years later, the National Amusement Device Company of Dayton constructed a small roller coaster, the Comet, Jr. The postwar years appear to have been profitable, and in 1946 the park welcomed a new Waffle Stand and a group of major rides that included the Flying

Fast and physically abusive, the Cyclone was popular with those who had the courage to ride it more than once.

When cross-town rival Luna Park closed in 1929, Gooding purchased Luna's magnificent four-abreast carousel. The carousel had been built by the Philadelphia Toboggan Company (Carousel #35) in 1915. After Puritas closed, it was moved to Indian Lake and still operates in Missouri.

The miniature train, a postwar addition to Puritas Springs Park, passed close to one of the hills of the Cyclone Coaster.

Among the rides in Kiddieland was an elaborately decorated car ride that included sporty automobiles and bright-red fire trucks. On the extreme right is the Blue Goose ride.

Scooters, Octopus, and Whip. A year later, the Allan Herschell Company delivered a number of kiddie rides to Puritas Springs Park. During the 1950s, Jungle Larry, who later became famous on Cleveland television, at Chippewa Lake Park, and at Cedar Point, established his "Circus Africa" at Puritas Springs Park.

Despite the postwar baby boom, Puritas Springs endured a series of problems, many caused by the treacherous Cyclone coaster. Although park official A. J. Ilg assured the public that the Cyclone was both safe and properly maintained, the company was forced to carry insurance policies that provided for $50,000 in coverage per

The Guess Your Weight booth was always popular, although the operator was an expert at guessing weight within a few pounds. Despite his skill, it was prudent to let a number of players win so that others would see prizes being carried around the park. Every games operator knows that winners displaying their prizes are the best type of advertising.

An aerial view of Puritas Springs Park revealed how the Cyclone coaster dipped deep into the ravine and wandered through a forest of mature trees. At night, most of the track was not illuminated, providing for a terrifying and surprising ride.

Always a big hit with younger children was the live pony ride. For many city kids, this ride was their first experience with an animal larger than the family dog.

accident. Unfortunately, the Puritas Springs Park Company needed every dollar of its insurance. In August of 1942, a young man was seriously injured when he was catapulted out of his seat on a curve and fell 40 feet to the ground. Then, during June and July of 1946, three women were injured on the Cyclone. Although none were thrown from the ride, the violent first drop fractured one woman's spine. The Cleveland Police Department ordered that the ride be closed and fully inspected. The insurance company, upset with the frequency of accidents but knowing little about the technology of roller coasters, suggested that the speed of the coaster train be reduced. The maligned Cyclone reopened, but in 1953, a twenty-one-year-old man fell from his car, was struck by the heavy, speeding train and died. Other mishaps also occurred at Puritas Springs. In 1945 a park employee was killed beneath the Tumble Bug ride, and on January 1, 1946, a fire destroyed the dance hall, leaving park owners stunned by $200,000 in fire damage, mostly to ride parts and food service equipment that had been stored in the basement of the building for the winter.

In 1947, Puritas Springs and Euclid Beach were the focus of unwanted publicity when the parks declared their roller rinks to be private clubs in order to exclude blacks. Despite fires, accidents, negative press, and the resulting decline in profits, Puritas Springs Park managed to struggle through the 1950s.

Clarence Behrendt, the park's major food concessionaire, feeds freshly made taffy into the machine that cut the candy to size and wrapped it. This 1950s photo was taken in the popcorn stand.

One of the new faces to appear at Puritas Springs after World War II was Clarence Behrendt. Behrendt had worked at Luna Park as a boy, and after serving in the army during the war he started the B & B Popcorn company, a distributor of popcorn, equipment, and supplies. In 1946, he was offered a concession contract to operate the popcorn stand at Puritas Springs, where he and his family served popcorn, caramel corn, peanuts, popcorn balls, and fabulous taffy. The Behrendt stand developed an enviable reputation for quality and cleanliness. In fact, the Goodings were so pleased with Clarence Behrendt's quality standards that he was approached to operate the park's cotton candy stand, hamburger stand, and frozen custard stand. It was a busy life for Behrendt and his family.

After taffy was wrapped, it was weighed and bagged. Here, Frank Behrendt prepares for a busy day in the popcorn stand.

I REMEMBER . . . My father, Clarence Behrendt, worked at Cleveland's Luna Park when he was young. After spending three years in the army, Dad came home and started Ellis Sales and B & B Popcorn. We used to make popcorn balls for schools.

It was 1946 or early 1947 when a friend of Dad's called and asked him to consider taking over the popcorn stand at Puritas Springs. We started in the spring of 1947, and Dad loved it. As the Goodings saw Dad work, they offered us the cotton candy stand and the hamburger stand . . . and eventually we had the custard stand.

My brother Frank and I were young when we started working. Frank was nine and I was ten when we were working at the park full-time.

"Pizza Al" and his family pose in his Pizza stand about 1950. Although the pizza ovens (right) created a great deal of heat and made the stand uncomfortable on hot days, pizza stands were always a lucrative venture.

The popcorn stand had popcorn, caramel corn, popcorn balls, peanuts, and taffy. Wonderful taffy!

The cotton candy stand (my stand) had cotton candy, candy apples, Sno Cones, and waffles. (That was the worst, sitting in front of hot grease and cooking waffles for hours at a time.)

The hamburger stand (Mom's stand) had hamburgers, hot dogs, French fries, coffee, and doughnuts. All our food was top notch. My dad prided himself on the best food and the cleanest stands.

The frozen custard stand was the last stand we had. Dad always added extra things to the mix to make it "ours." And the people loved it.

The park became our home from Easter Sunday to Labor Day. We would open at 11 A.M. and close at 11 P.M. Those people employed by the Goodings full-time almost became family. Two who were especially close were Harry Knox and Lottie Adelson. They were very special people.

For years we could almost set our clock by the huge golden lab-mix dog that was known to travel up the hill from the valley. It seemed he really enjoyed the custard at the frozen custard stand. About 7 P.M. every evening he would make his way through the front gate, go directly to the custard stand, and sit and wait for his treat.

The cotton candy stand sold both fluffy cotton candy and crispy French waffles. In the last years of the park, Joyce Behrendt fries waffles in preparation for the day's business.

We had several park policemen, but the one that got the attention of everyone was Big Al. One of his jobs was to make sure that no liquor was brought into the park. One evening a couple of men were in a huddle near my stand. Al walked up to them and was talking to them when he reached for his nightstick and as quick as a wink hit all of them in the pants pockets. I heard CRACK, CRACK, CRACK, and liquid dripped to the ground from their pants. I heard them exclaim as they left the park, "Honest, I don't know where that came from."

There were wonderful picnics at the park. The ethnic picnics were the best. It was neat to see the girls and boys dressed in the old-world costumes and hear their music and see their dances.

One of the most riotous groups was the postal employees' picnic. Somehow a group of these men, who were leading a donkey around the park, came to the bus stop gate near the cotton candy stand. They decided that the donkey had to go for a bus ride. They shoved, pulled, and pushed the donkey into the bus with the driver yelling and trying to block its path. Well, they got it on the bus, and then couldn't get it off. It was stuck in the back of the bus. And you know what happens when a donkey gets scared, don't you? Needless to say, they had to take the bus back to the barns, get the donkey out, and clean up the mess.

Jungle Larry and Safari Jack had a jungle show the last few years the park was open. They milked poisonous snakes and had big lion dogs, lion cubs, and tiger cubs. They also had some monkeys that had very large, sharp fangs. One night one of the monkeys tore into one of the cubs and put a nasty gash in its shoulder. My husband, Lee, who was my boyfriend at the time, was called to duty to hold the cub while Jack stitched the wound. Thankfully, Jack knew how to sew and had given the cat a sedative, but they still weren't sure how soon the cat would awaken. — *Joyce Behrendt Biddulph*

"The park became our home from Easter Sunday to Labor Day. We would open at 11 A.M. and close at 11 P.M."

Another perennial park employee was Harry Knox, seen here working in Clarence Behrendt's hot dog stand. Knox also operated rides, sold tickets, and did whatever other jobs needed to be done.

The Japanese String Game, like the Fish Pond, guaranteed a prize every time. These games, which required luck but not skill, were especially popular with children.

To combat declining business at the park, manager Jim Gooding increased spending for advertising and planned numerous promotions to draw patrons. Many weekends would find Cleveland Indians baseball stars and television personalities appearing at Puritas Springs Park. Jungle Larry presented his Circus Africa show daily, and in 1957 four new rides were installed to entice customers. But even these efforts failed to increase business. It seemed that the age of the family amusement park had come to an end.

Finally, in 1958, the Gooding family made the difficult decision to close Puritas Springs Park. The beautiful carousel was moved to San Juan Resort on Indian Lake in western Ohio; later it was moved again to St. Louis, where it still operates. The once fearsome Cyclone coaster stood idle until it was razed in 1960. Other parts of the park were sold, razed, or destroyed in a fire that occurred on May 10, 1959. Eventually, the parklands were developed as a residential community, and Puritas Springs Park was all but forgotten—unless you happened to glance down into the ravine, where tenacious remnants of the Cyclone's mighty structure could still be seen more than forty years after the park closed.

By the mid-1920s, most parks were starting to install kiddielands to entertain the youngest visitors. One of Puritas Springs's most charming kiddie rides was The Blue Goose, a favorite with children for years.

Amusement park kiddielands operated two types of boat rides, wet boats and dry boats. The dry boats operated on a track, while wet boats (shown in this photo) actually floated in a tank of water.

Although most Ohio parks closed for the season in September, maintenance crews and the group sales staff worked through the winter to be ready for the coming summer. During the off-season, rides and equipment were rebuilt and repainted, and in spring outdoor facilities were given a fresh coat of paint.

I REMEMBER . . . I worked part of a summer, probably 1956 or 1957, at the cotton candy, popcorn, and drink stand that was over the footbridge to the skating rink and by the kiddie rides.

As the years went by the park fell into negative repute. They didn't sell alcoholic beverages at the park, but people gossiped that many drinkers went there and it developed a sort of unsavory reputation.

There was a penny arcade with many old (even then) pinball machines that used only two pennies placed side by side to play.

The park had an outstanding carousel and a skating rink in the back that was very popular and stayed open a few years after the amusement section closed.

While the park was on a much smaller scale than the other parks in the area, the Cyclone coaster made it happen. I had relatives who were regulars at Euclid Beach, and they admitted, as I knew, that the Cyclone was a more exciting ride. It was a dark and foreboding ride at night, and was surrounded by large trees whose branches looked like they would hit you just before you dropped under them.

They had another, rather odd, ride that I'd seen nowhere else. It was called the Moon Racer, where a small train of cars shaped like a rocket ship sped around a large tilted disk. — *James Baesel*

The 1950s and 1960s witnessed the closing of most of America's great and not-so-great amusement parks. A "Keep Out" sign was the final greeting to those who passed the closed park after the 1958 season.

Cleveland's Other Parks

While the largest amusement facilities dominated, there were also a number of smaller facilities that managed to operate successfully in and around Cleveland. Some lasted for many years, while others were short-lived and disappeared almost without a trace. Scenic Park, Lincoln Park, Willoughbeach Park, and Orchard Lake Park were among the Cleveland-area parks that were quickly forgotten after their demise.

Scenic Park, which claimed to have owned one of the country's first Scenic Railway roller coasters, was situated along the right-of-way of the Rocky River Railroad near Clifton Boulevard. Although Scenic Park was known to have attracted as many as fifteen thousand visitors in 1905, it was ultimately unable to keep pace with the larger parks.

Lincoln Park opened in June 1906, on the site of the former Scenic Park. Admission was only one nickel, and Lincoln Park claimed to offer more free attractions than all of the other area parks combined. Emulating Luna Park in many ways, the park featured a roller coaster, circle swing, Japanese Village, Egyptian Hall, and various other amusements. Although it opened with a flourish, Lincoln Park never proved a serious threat to Euclid Beach, Luna Park, or Puritas Springs Park.

☜

During the 1950s, Kiddie Playland was located on Northfield Road near where Randall Park Mall now stands. The largest ride was an Allan Herschell Little Dipper, an all-steel roller coaster built specifically for kiddielands.

The city's 100-acre Woodland Hills Park was added to the Cleveland park system in 1900. By the 1920s, the park operated a large public swimming pool that competed with the nearby facilities at Luna Park.

Willoughbeach Park, situated 15 miles east of Public Square, was easily reached via the fast electric cars of the Cleveland, Painesville & Eastern Railway. It was a fairly small park and closed when the electric railway ceased operations.

Gordon Park, originally privately owned and later a city park, was never an amusement park. It did, however, offer an excellent bathhouse and pavilion, Lake Erie swimming, and shady picnic areas.

Recognizing the popularity of amusement parks, the Cleveland, Painesville & Eastern interurban railway opened Willoughbeach Park in 1907. It was situated on Lake Shore Boulevard near where the Shoregate Shopping Center later was constructed. The CP&E ran from Euclid Avenue to Painesville, placing Willoughbeach Park within easy reach of thousands of Greater Clevelanders. Located on the Lake Erie shore, Willoughbeach Park offered patrons a variety of entertainments

and amusements including lake bathing, dancing in the spacious ballroom, and an ornate carousel, among other diversions. Like Euclid beach, Willoughbeach was a "dry" park. However, the absence of alcohol did not dissuade the residents of Collinwood from holding their first annual community outing at Willoughbeach.

The early twenties were prosperous for the CP&E, which carried 3,250,000 passengers in 1920 alone. Accordingly, the company spent a great deal of money in 1924 to upgrade and improve the park. A new roller coaster was constructed, the ballroom was redone, and the baseball diamond and picnic grove were expanded. For the 1925 season an Automobile Coaster was installed. This new attraction enabled riders to drive their own cars along a large roller coaster–like structure. On the surface it may have seemed as though things were going well for Willoughbeach Park, but in 1926 the number of CP&E riders slipped to 400,000. Faced with declining patronage and profits, the CP&E abandoned interurban operations, and they did not open Willoughbeach Park for the 1926 season. Attempts to sell Willoughbeach Park were unsuccessful, and the park stood vacant for a while before being razed.

On Memorial Day weekend of 1927, Orchard Lake Park opened for business at the corner of Northfield and Peninsula Roads, south of Cleveland. Advertised as "A Refined Park for Refined People," Orchard Lake was operated by Thomas E. Thorpe, who had previously managed Indian Lake Park at Russells Point in

☞

The Great Lakes Exposition of 1936–37, located on the lakeshore of Cleveland, was not an amusement park. It did, however, have a complete amusement section and an area known as Streets of the World. The 10-acre "Streets" represented thirty-three nationalities and included 186 buildings. Most popular were the cafes of the Italian Village and the French Casino.

Another city-owned facility that competed with the area's amusement parks was Edgewater Park. Located at West 58th Street, the park was acquired by the city in 1894 and offered swimming, baseball, playgrounds, and picnic areas. After being neglected for years, it became Cleveland Lakefront State Park in 1978.

Dorothy Ann Palliotet of Akron and movie comedian Charley Chase pose in front of the carousel at the Great Lakes Exposition on July 3, 1936. The carousel appears to be a Spillman Engineering Company product.

☞

western Ohio. Orchard Lake Park covered 40 acres and boasted a parking lot that could accommodate ten thousand cars, a spring-fed lake, picnic groves, baseball diamonds, and a small lineup of rides. Although there was no roller coaster, the park did operate a carousel, Ferris wheel, Merry Mix-Up, and miniature railroad. The Dancing Pavilion was advertised as "one of the largest and most beautiful" in Ohio and hosted Carlone's ten-piece orchestra during the 1927 season. It appears that Orchard Lake Park was one of the unlucky facilities that failed to survive the early years of the Great Depression.

After the recession of 1920–21 abated, there was a nationwide surge in the number of new amusement parks. The fact that most of the country was already saturated with parks did little to deter those who were counting on their investments to produce big profits. In 1922, Cleveland certainly had a more than adequate number of parks. The traditional favorites—Euclid Beach, Luna Park, and Puritas Springs—were large enough to handle the summer crowds coming from Cleveland neighborhoods. Furthermore, numerous other parks were well within traveling distance from Cleveland. To the west were Sandusky's Cedar Point and Vermilion's Crystal Beach Park. A pleasant drive east would bring patrons to Mentor's Playland, Geneva-on-the-Lake, Woodland Beach, and Willoughbeach. And in nearby Medina County, Chippewa Lake Park and its adjacent cottage communities were attracting many Clevelanders. In addition, Akron's Summit Beach Park, Canton's Meyers Lake Park, and Youngstown's Idora Park also drew patrons from Cleveland. With all of these parks from which to choose, it seemed that there was little justification for building another Cleveland park. Nevertheless, the owners of Gordon Gardens moved beyond the planning stage late in 1922.

Gordon Gardens was built opposite Gordon Park at East 72nd Street, a location that was very close to both Euclid Beach Park and Luna Park. Obviously, any new park would have had a difficult time trying to compete with these well-run, beloved parks.

Charles P. Salen, operator of food concessions at Luna Park, also obtained a license to vend foods and beverages at Gordon Gardens. Salen had strong ties to the public recreation industry. As director of public works for the city of Cleveland, he con-

The Big Dipper at Gordon Gardens was owned by Robert Loehr, who also owned amusement devices at Luna Park and elsewhere. In addition to the coaster, Loehr also operated a carousel, Whip, Caterpillar, Circle Swing, and a few other rides at Gordon Gardens.

Gordon Gardens was one of the area's short-lived parks, opening on Memorial Day of 1923 and closing after the 1927 season. The large Big Dipper roller coaster was designed by John A. Miller and built by Miller & Baker, Inc., of New York.

structed baseball diamonds, sponsored skating races, built a skating rink near Edgewater Park, and promoted ice carnivals. During the 1890s, he and Jake Mintz began operating concessions at ballparks, and the two men became important concessionaires at Luna.

Robert Loehr, a major ride owner at Luna Park, was also deeply involved in Gordon Gardens. Loehr was granted exclusive rights to install and operate amusement rides at the new park. When Gordon Gardens opened on Memorial Day of 1923, Loehr unveiled John A. Miller's Big Dipper roller coaster, a carousel, Whip, Airplane Swing, Caterpillar, and a few other rides. The park also offered the usual game and food stands, a shooting gallery, a motordrome, a dance pavilion, and a stage for band concerts.

Almost from the beginning, Gordon Gardens seemed to be operating under a dark cloud. On July 22, 1923, an eighteen-year-old boy was killed instantly when he leaned over the front of the train on the Big Dipper roller coaster and fell in

Built on the site of Scenic Park, Lincoln Park opened in Rocky River during June of 1906. This view shows various park attractions including the Circle Swing, carousel building, roller coaster, and a number of buildings. Lincoln Park was never a serious competitor to either Luna Park or Euclid Beach.

front of the speeding train. Coaster accidents rarely injure park business, as large numbers of curious adventurers seem to visit parks after accidents. However, Gordon Gardens needed all the positive publicity it could gather. Despite the expertise and experience of Salen and Loehr, Gordon Gardens never managed to attract large crowds and failed to compete with the older and larger parks. As the city of Cleveland began developing the lakefront, it purchased Gordon Gardens for $365,000 in August 1927. The park was not razed immediately, but suspicious fires destroyed a number of buildings over the next few years and eventually all trace of Gordon Gardens disappeared.

While the brief lives of these parks left little to remember them by, other Cleveland-area establishments rendered more lasting impressions.

Just a few miles east of Cleveland was Mentor Beach Playland. Although a fairly small park, it catered to the thousands of people who visited the lakeshore during the summer months. The ride just inside of the main entrance is a very early model of the popular Tilt-A-Whirl.

White City

In the spring of 1905, the Cleveland *Plain Dealer* reported that "Not only has the amusement park lightning struck Cleveland hard this summer, but it has struck twice." Reporters added that "Such a diversity of sights and amusements has never before been seen in the Forest City." Cleveland's burgeoning amusement park industry saw a lot of action during the winter of 1904–05. Both Luna Park and White City were rushed to completion in readiness for the coming summer season.

While Luna Park was modeled after Coney Island's Luna in New York, White City was created in the image of another Coney Island facility, the beautiful Dreamland Park (1904–1911). Dreamland was one of the most magnificent parks ever conceived. Originally costing $2,500,000 to build, Dreamland literally glowed with the wattage of one million electric light bulbs. During the summer Dreamland employed fourteen thousand to handle crowds of up to sixty thousand people.

Edward C. Boyce, president of White City in Cleveland, also owned two attractions at Dreamland in New York: the "Under and Over the Sea" and the "Destruc-

tion of Pompeii." No doubt Boyce's experiences with Dreamland and its concessionaires came in handy when he decided to erect White City Park on the site of
Cleveland's short-lived Manhattan Beach Park.

One successful publicity gimmick employed by Dreamland was to interest
well-known theatrical performers in owning and operating concessions at the
park. In theory, their presence at the park would attract both crowds and newspaper coverage. Irish comedian Andrew Mack owned the Fish Pond game, and
Broadway actress Marie Dressler ran the popcorn and roasted peanut operations.
Boyce utilized the same concept at White City, convincing Miss Dressler to install
the Bump the Bumps ride. However, Coney Island was a lot closer to Broadway
than was Cleveland, and Dressler found little time to make personal appearances
at White City.

Boyce also borrowed White City's design and color scheme from Dreamland.
Striving for a classic, refined ambiance, Boyce had all of his park's buildings
painted a sparkling, pristine white. Although Dreamland later changed its colors

White City's management
placed a horseshoe-
shaped awning around
the Shoot-the-Chutes
lagoon to shelter visitors
who enjoyed watching
the boats splash into the
water. The bridge over
the Chutes also provided
an excellent vantage
point for observing the
speeding boats.

to cream and red to attract more attention, in Cleveland, White City remained forever faithful to its name.

White City's entrance on East 140th Street was a simple white arch with the words "The White City" emblazoned in lights. A Shoot-the-Chutes ride was at the center of the park, and each boat was named in honor of a nearby city, such as Collinwood and Cleveland. The rapidly descending boats were the first sight that greeted visitors after they paid their ten-cent admission fee and passed through the entrance arch. The Café, situated just west of the Chutes structure, offered upscale cuisine served al fresco. To the east of the Chutes was a spacious ballroom with room for three thousand dancers and open sides to welcome lake breezes on warm nights.

Edward Boyce also borrowed other ideas from Dreamland in New York. For instance Dreamland headliner Frank Bostock was persuaded to install another of his wild animal shows at White City. And Dr. Martin Couney, a pioneer in the care of premature babies, duplicated his Dreamland baby incubator exhibit at White City. Dr. Couney constructed a small hospital to receive premature babies, installed incubators of his own invention in climate-controlled exhibit areas, and employed wet nurses to provide mother's milk. The parents of the premature babies were never charged for his services, and the operation was totally funded by a ten-cent-per-person admission charge. During his lifetime, Dr. Couney saved 6,500 of the 8,000 premature babies entrusted to his care at Coney Island, Atlantic City, and at other locations.

From the top of White City's Shoot-the-Chutes ride, the view included the ballroom (left), the open-sided Café and Restaurant (right), and the Laughing Gallery fun house (right center). To the left of the entrance was the station for the Scenic Railway roller coaster.

"White City", Cleveland, Ohio.

Although some aspects of this postcard view were greatly exaggerated, White City was a very impressive park when it opened in 1905. Located at East 140th Street, White City, like Euclid Beach and Luna Park, relied on the Cleveland streetcar system to deliver patrons to its gates.

Another Dreamland concept that showed up at White City was Sir Hiram Maxim's Flying Airships. Maxim, an explosives expert who invented the machine gun, developed a massive captive airplane ride that was first tested in England before Dreamland purchased one of the few United States installations. Of course, Boyce had to have one of Maxim's huge machines in Cleveland. The ride stood 150 feet tall and cost $75,000 to install. A carousel, Scenic Railway, free circus, fun house, and various other rides, as well as games and food stands, rounded out White City's offerings.

Boyce must have been pleased with the results of the first season's operation. With streetcars stopping directly in front of the admission gate, White City drew huge crowds. To bolster attendance on slow weekdays, women and children were admitted free until 3 P.M. On July 2, 1905, White City counted 25,000 visitors, compared with 22,000 at Luna and 30,000 at Euclid Beach. In September, White City ended a very successful inaugural season, and Boyce looked forward to the summer of 1906.

The winter of 1905–06 was spent installing a new pumping system to transport Lake Erie water to the top of the Shoot-the-Chutes. This allowed fresh water to cascade down the ride's incline and also helped maintain fresher water in the lagoon. As the opening day of May 26, 1906, approached, the Rossi Brothers were hired to provide a massive fireworks display to signal the start of a new summer season. Unfortunately, the brothers would not have the opportunity to exhibit their pyrotechnic skills.

On Friday, May 25, workers were applying hot tar in the tunnel of the Old Mill boat ride. At 11:15 A.M. the tar caught fire, and within minutes the interior of the Old Mill was engulfed in flames. Early amusement parks were tinderboxes, built of wood, lath, and staff and coated with highly flammable paints. In two hours, the flames spread throughout White City, reducing everything except the Scenic Railway to ashes. Fortunately, the baby incubators were not yet occupied, and Bostock's animals were still in transit to the park. Gone were thirty concessions, the Café, Bostock's arena, the Shoot-the-Chutes, the ballroom, and the power-house. Losses were estimated at $200,000, with only $60,000 covered by insurance. Undeterred, Boyce vowed to rebuild.

After a year of rebuilding, a new White City opened in late June of 1907. The spectacular rides, like Maxim's airplanes and the Shoot-the-Chutes, were nowhere to be seen. The new White City was less ostentatious and far less costly than the

White City was struck by a savage windstorm that tossed ticket booths 50 feet in the air, flattened small buildings, and tore the roofs from the larger structures.

original park. A new ballroom and restaurant had been constructed, and exhibits included an Indian Village and a wild animal show. Although the Shoot-the-Chutes had not been rebuilt, the lagoon remained as a home for sea lions.

On July 24, 1907, White City was struck by a savage windstorm that tossed ticket booths 50 feet in the air, flattened small buildings, and tore the roofs from the larger structures. The volcano in Pain's Pompeii firework show totally collapsed. As the saying goes, "The show must go on!" and that same day Pain presented his pyrotechnic exhibition minus the storm-flattened erupting mountain. Physically, White City recovered from the storm damage, but attendance never reached the 1905 levels. Hoping to draw crowds, White City opened in 1908 with a free admission gate. Unfortunately, free admission did little to attract crowds to White City when nearby Euclid Beach and Luna Park offered more rides and better attractions.

Although it ultimately failed, White City drew huge crowds of curious Clevelanders during its inaugural season. On July 4, 1905, it was estimated that 85,000 people passed through the park's gates.

After a disappointing 1908 season, White City was sold to new owners and opened in 1909 as Cleveland Beach Park. The Scenic Railway from 1905 remained, as well as the sparkling-white painted buildings. The dozen or so rides included a carousel, the Mystic River, and the Circle Swing. Cleveland Beach Park promoted band concerts, Pain's fireworks, "polite" vaudeville, and even Polar Bears. In June, the curious came to see the "new" park, but there was no way that Cleveland Beach would succeed any better than White City in competing with the other local parks.

The unfortunate park, however, was not dead. In 1911, it again opened, this time as Bay Park. With a free gate, the park claimed that Trostler's $100,000 Scenic Ballroom was the most wonderful dancing facility on earth. It also claimed fifty attractions, which included motorboat racing, the Jungle, Whitmark's Temple of Music, the Venetian Boulevard, the El Sharinik Silk Exhibit, and the Slavonic Troubadours. With no more success than Cleveland Beach, Bay Park soon closed also. Bay Park's owners simply stated that the park never "caught on" with the public.

In 1921, White City opened once more, this time as a campground and picnic facility for disabled servicemen from the First World War. Eventually, the Easterly Sewage Disposal facility was built on the land once occupied by White City.

Ironically, White City's inspiration, Dreamland Park, also had an unfortunate history. A spectacular fire completely destroyed the park during the early morning hours of May 27, 1911. Eerily like the earlier White City fire, it started when workmen were applying hot tar inside a boat ride tunnel.

Memphis Kiddie Park

Very visible from the street, Memphis Kiddie Park was an instant success. Clean, well maintained, and properly managed, Memphis Kiddie Park is the epitome of America's best kiddie parks.

Stuart Wintner was a Cleveland accountant who developed an interest in the amusement industry while reading *Billboard* magazines at the office of one of his clients (until *Amusement Business* began publication, *Billboard* was the nation's major amusement publication for park operators). Although he had no interest in trying to compete with Euclid Beach or Puritas Springs, Wintner saw the potential for a children's park on the west side of Cleveland. He acquired land on Memphis Avenue in Brooklyn and contracted with the Allan Herschell Company of North Tonawanda, New York, for new kiddie rides. At the time, Allan Herschell was one of the oldest and largest manufacturers of park rides in the world.

In the spring of 1952, the rides arrived at the park site and assembly began. In addition to the Allan Herschell rides, which included a carousel and Little Dipper roller coaster, Wintner also purchased a miniature Ferris wheel and a fleet of Hodges Cars, which were propelled by the brute strength of the young rider's arms.

Opening day, 1952 was especially momentous for Stuart Wintner because his son Russell was born the very same day. Since then, the five-acre park has become a traditional summer recreation site serving three generations of northern Ohioans. Asked about the park's formula for success, Russell Winter answered, "The park never tried to be what it was not. We never changed the appearance of the park and always remembered that our goal was to make younger children happy."

In 2004, the 1952 Little Dipper roller coaster was the oldest all-steel coaster operating in the United States. In June of 2004, the American Coaster Enthusiasts included a visit to the Little Dipper during their annual convention, spending a full day at Memphis Kiddie Park.

Memphis Kiddie Park has never charged for admission or parking, and ride tickets are very affordable. Over time, a food operation, arcade, and miniature golf course were added, as were live ponies and an archery range (although the latter two were later discontinued).

Late in 1952, Paul Wintner, who was also involved with the park, began plans to construct the Memphis Drive-In Theater near the park. Designed to handle a thousand cars, the new theater cost an estimated $200,000 and continues to be a popular West Side attraction during the warmer months.

Encouraged by the success of Memphis Kiddie Park, Stuart Wintner opened an indoor kiddie park in Philadelphia. In 1965 the Philadelphia park was closed,

For a number of years, Memphis Kiddie Park operated a live pony ride (left). As the park was expanded, the live ponies were phased out of the operation.

For half a century, the miniaturized rides at Memphis Kiddie Park have brought smiles to the faces of thousands of northern Ohio youngsters. Many visitors are now third-generation patrons of the park.

and the rides moved to Columbus, where Wintner operated a kiddie park for a few years. Wintner also built a number of themed miniature golf courses at various locations. Among the most interesting was an Oriental-themed course built next to the Andress Drive-In on Broadway in Maple Heights.

For more than fifty years, Memphis Kiddie Park has managed to survive when scores of other amusement parks, large and small, have closed their gates. Current management continues to operate Memphis Kiddie Park according to Stuart Wintner's original concept, serving the families of Cleveland and surrounding communities with a charming, well-maintained facility.

From the day the park opened, the boat ride has been a favorite with the younger riders. Fifty years after they were built, rides like this have still not lost their charm.

At the entrance to Memphis Kiddie Park, guests crossed the miniature railroad track. To the left is a 1952 Allan Herschell carousel, which is still in operation at the park.

By midsummer, with the hotels and cottages full, the beaches of Geneva-on-the-Lake were filled with bathers and sun worshipers. In the evenings, the sunburned visitors visited the numerous amusements and shops along Main Street.

Geneva-on-the-Lake

East of Cleveland, along Lake Erie's shore, is the charming resort community of Geneva-on-the-Lake. Unlike Euclid Beach or Luna Park, Geneva-on-the-Lake is truly a summer resort—an enclave of independently owned amusements and accommodations clustered around the town and along the lakeshore. Operating within this resort community is Erieview amusement park.

Geneva-on-the-Lake is among Ohio's oldest summer resorts. On July 4, 1869, Cullen Spencer and Edwin Pratt opened Sturgeon Point, a small picnic grounds that boasted a small carousel. Before long, a campground developed on the site. Food services followed, and L. C. Spencer operated the resort's first dancing pavilion as well as Rose Cottage, the area's first indoor overnight accommodations. Eventually, as more and more people journeyed to Geneva-on-the-Lake, additional accommodations appeared, including the Shady Beach Hotel, the exclusive Colonial Hotel, the Allen Court Cottages, and the Erie Side Cottages.

The Shady Beach Hotel opened its doors in 1896, catering to "select clientele only," meaning that only white patrons of Western European lineage were welcome to stay there. The Shady Beach stubbornly maintained this policy well into the 1950s, and those who "qualified" for a room probably enjoyed a pleasant stay. All rooms were large and airy, and the best rooms, equipped with private baths, rented for $60 a week. In addition to the pleasures of Lake Erie, guests at the

In this 1930s view of Geneva-on-the-Lake's main street, cars are parked in front of Pera's New Inn (left) and the adjacent novelty store, which supplied visitors with bathing and tennis needs, refreshments, souvenirs, cigars, and cigarettes.

Shady Beach could enjoy on-premises tennis, badminton, ping-pong, shuffleboard, and croquet. Marketing an exhilarating experience, the hotel sought visitors who "like the feel of a breeze on your cheeks," enticing them to "come down and let old man Lake Erie tone you up."

While the little resort, now called Geneva-on-the-Lake, was popular with locals, it was not readily accessible to people from Cleveland, Akron, Youngstown, Pittsburgh, or Erie until the advent of the automobile. Then, thanks largely to the family car, Geneva-on-the-Lake became a popular summer retreat for weary

The Casino Ballroom was built in 1912 and became the entertainment centerpiece at Geneva-on-the-Lake. At the height of interest in Florida as a winter resort venue, Joe Sheehan and His Miami Beach Orchestra were a big hit at the Casino.

city dwellers. Soon the resort offered two dozen hotels or boardinghouses and scores of summer cottages. In 1912, the Casino Ballroom opened its doors, and Geneva-on-the-Lake's transformation from tiny summer community to full-scale amusement resort was under way. The Casino, owned by Glick and Johnson, was an immediate success and had to be expanded for the busy 1918 season.

After the First World War, a mobile population with disposable income descended on Geneva-on-the-Lake in search of fun and entertainment. Swimming, fishing, tennis, dancing, boating, and all the usual pastimes associated with sum-

Marketing an exhilarating experience, the hotel sought visitors who "like the feel of a breeze on your cheeks," enticing them to "come down and let old man Lake Erie tone you up."

mer resorts were available at Geneva-on-the-Lake. Pera's Pier Ballroom was built in 1928, and the construction of cottages, hotels, and retail establishments to serve visitors proceeded at a brisk pace. That same year the Woodward family opened the new Breakers Ballroom, and a few seasons later the Perogla Gardens debuted.

Like Atlantic City and other resorts, Geneva-on-the-Lake also developed a thriving cottage community. While many of these cottages were privately owned and for family use, others were rented by the week or for the entire season.

Busy Geneva-on-the-Lake, Ohio

The postwar baby boom brought new prosperity to Geneva-on-the-Lake. Main Street was thronged with buildings housing games, pizza parlors, refreshment stands, souvenir and novelty shops, and scores of advertising signs.

Sustained in part by dance marathons at the Perogla Gardens, Geneva-on-the-Lake struggled through the Great Depression, but was faced with decreased numbers of visitors and reduced spending. There was, however, some activity during the difficult years of the 1930s. About 1935, R. A. Gregory constructed a large, three-story bathing pavilion and a water toboggan that slid daring bathers into the lake from a towering slide. Unfortunately, the facility was destroyed by fire after just a few seasons. Around the time of this fire, carnival impresario Floyd Gooding installed a carousel that was apparently not a financial success and only lasted one season.

The advent of the Big Band Era and the unique economy of the Second World War, however, brought recovery, and Geneva-on-the-Lake, unlike many resorts, survived and retained its charm through the remainder of the twentieth century and into the new century. Many of the country's major dance bands included Geneva-on-the-Lake on their summer tours of amusement park and resort ballrooms, and, according to tradition, bandleader Kay Kyser spent the better part of a summer living in the attic of the Shady Beach Hotel.

As was the case at every resort or amusement park, a single person or family exerted a great deal of influence on the success of the resort. At Geneva-on-the-Lake, it has been the Pera family. E. M. "Pop" Pera had worked at New York's Wal-

Compared to the Casino, Pera's 1928 Pier Ballroom was spacious and airy. The Pier Ballroom included a more elaborate stage, mood-setting lighting, and a crystal ball that cast flashing specks of light around the dance floor.

Eddie's Grill has been a
landmark on Main Street
in Geneva-on-the-Lake
since it opened in 1950.
For more than fifty years,
it has been the place
to meet friends, eat, or
just watch the passing
crowds.

dorf-Astoria Hotel and at a resort hotel in Jacksonville, Florida, before opening
his own restaurant in downtown Cleveland. After a Sunday visit to Geneva-on-
the-Lake with his wife, Martha, Pera fell in love with the lakeside community. In
1921, they sold their Cleveland restaurant and moved to the resort, purchasing the
New Inn. The New Inn, which was built in 1903, was a small, twenty-two-room
hotel with a dining room on the main floor. The new owners built a tennis court
in 1922 and a miniature golf course in 1923, and established a recreation area
behind the hotel called "Pera's Park." At the time, Pera's Park was little more than
a shady area providing access to the beach.

After Pera built the Pier Ballroom in 1928, it was becoming clear that he was
about to become an amusement entrepreneur. First, he opened a series of Skee
Ball alleys next to the Casino Ballroom. Then, in 1940, he constructed a new Dodgem building. When the Second World War interfered with plans, the Dodgem
building was converted in a large game building bearing the sign: "Recreation
for the Nation." When the war ended, a complete set of cars was shipped from
the Dodgem Corporation, and the games were replaced with the popular electric
vehicles.

Recognizing what the postwar baby boom could mean to the amusement industry, Pera determined to build his own amusement park by the lake. Perhaps
influenced by the success of the Flying Scooters at Euclid Beach, he installed one
of these rides on his property in 1947. After that, new rides appeared almost yearly.
In 1948, new kiddie rides were installed, and in 1955 the park was dubbed "Pera's
Kiddieland."

By the 1970s, an aging, but nonetheless active, "Pop" Pera (he died in 1984)
sought to attract more adult patrons by installing additional major rides. The

Octopus ride that had been added in 1958 was joined in the 1970s and '80s by a Roll-O-Plane, Tilt-A-Whirl, Paratrooper, National Amusement miniature rail-road, and a junior roller coaster. When Pittsburgh's West View Park closed in 1977, the Peras bought a group of Dodgem-like Lusse Auto Scooters and The Fright Zone, a 1963 ride-through dark ride. In 1980, the expanded park became Erieview Park.

By the early 2000s, the descendants of Pop Pera were still helping to preserve the quaint atmosphere of an old-fashioned summer resort at Geneva-on-the-Lake. Some of the Pera operations include an eighteen-ride amusement park, the Wild Water Works park, Woody's World Arcade, the Times Square Restaurant, Pera's Motel Suites, and the Swiss Chalet Nightclub.

Eddie's Grill is a legendary food establishment located on the main drag in Ge-neva-on-the-Lake. Eddie's has changed very little since it opened in 1950. Legions of fans still anxiously await one of Eddie's old-fashioned counter stools. From this vantage point they satisfy their hunger while watching resort life pass by.

Another Geneva-on-the-Lake attraction is the oldest continuously operating miniature golf course in the country. Opened in 1924 by Jack and Mary Aspin, it was purchased by the Allison family in 1981. The original course was made of clay and sand, requiring employees to level the "fairways" throughout the day with heavy rollers. The Allisons have maintained the traditions of the charming, historic golf course, and it is much the same as it was in the 1920s. A food stand, lemonade stand, and T-shirt shop near the golf course are also owned by the Al-lison family.

Overcoming the civil unrest and adverse publicity it and other resorts experi-enced in the turbulent 1960s, Geneva-on-the-Lake has reclaimed its place as one of the country's few remaining traditional lakeside summer resorts. For thousands of Clevelanders, it remains a favorite summer recreation spot.

When Pittsburgh's West View Park closed, Erieview Park acquired one of only three dark rides constructed by the Allan Herschell Company (and the only one still operating). It replaced the park's aging Pretzel dark ride.

Cleveland Zoo Kiddie Park

Founded in 1882, the Cleveland Zoo is the seventh-oldest zoological park in the United States. Originally opened in Wade Park on 73 acres donated by Jeptha Wade, it was moved to its current location in 1907.

The decade of the 1950s was one of substantial growth for the Cleveland Zoo. Launching its own African safari, the zoo brought back to Cleveland three elephants, two hippos, two rhinos, three giraffes, and many other animals. At that time it was popular for zoos to try a variety of means to entertain as well as educate visitors. One way they found was to add rides. For example, the Cincinnati Zoo installed a full-sized carousel, and many other facilities installed miniature trains, amusement rides, and even fully equipped kiddie sections.

The Petting Farm at the Cleveland Zoo was meant both to educate and to give urban and suburban children a chance to meet friendly farm animals.

The Toonerville Trolley, based on a comic strip of the early twentieth century, was a popular kiddie ride in many parks during the 1950s. Electrically powered, it operated on a single rail and meandered through the zoo's park.

 The Allan Herschell
Company built pony
cart rides for decades,
and they were among
the most popular of
kiddieland rides. In the
background is an Allan
Herschell carousel.

The Cleveland Zoo
Railroad operated an
excellent miniature diesel
locomotive and passenger
cars built by the
Miniature Train Company.
It was the same model of
train operated at Euclid
Beach Park until 1969.

Allan Herschell's Helicopter Ride actually gave riders some degree of control. A bar located in front of riders allowed them to raise and lower the copters in flight.

The Cleveland Zoo started out by installing an early miniature diesel train from the Miniature Train Company. The popularity of the little train soon led to the purchase of a group of new kiddie rides from the Allan Herschell Company.

Even though it was popular with younger visitors and their parents, future plans for the zoo and its expansion did not include the kiddieland. By the 1970s, the cost of maintaining the aging rides had become prohibitive. Ultimately, the kiddieland at the zoo was closed, surviving only as a happy memory for thousands of children who visited the park during the 1950s, '60s and '70s.

Long before the zoo constructed its kiddieland, it operated a gasoline-powered miniature railroad. Apparently modeled after the Burlington Zephyr of the 1930s, the little engine appears to have been a twelve-inch-gauge line.

Acknowledgments

No book is a solitary effort, and every author depends on others to provide information, guidance, advice, and materials. This book is no exception, and we wish to thank the many people and organizations that made it possible.

Lee Bush and Richard Hershey set the standard for all books about amusement parks when they published their first volume on Euclid Beach Park. Authors, historians, publishers, and lovers of the amusement park, Lee and Dick generously shared photos and information from their collection of materials about Cleveland parks. We are deeply thankful for their help, knowledge, friendship, and professionalism.

Among the many people who provided assistance and support were Georgette Allison, James Baesel, Christine Bailey, Marlene Zoul Benjamin, Joyce Biddulph, Richard L. Bowker, Dudley S. Humphrey, Jr., Marge Milliken, Marshall Moore, Esther Newman, Christine Porter, Jean Rumbold, Jim Seman, Eddie Sezon, John F. Szuch, Russell J. Wintner, and Don Woodward.

A number of companies and organizations also provided invaluable assistance. Included were the Aurora Historical Society, Cleveland Metroparks Zoo, Cleveland State University, Erieview Park, Geauga Lake, Geneva-on-the-Lake Convention and Visitors Bureau, the Humphrey Company, Memphis Kiddie Park, and the Western Reserve Historical Society.

To all who helped make this book possible, we are deeply indebted.

For Further Reading

Boas, Karen, and Ray Boas. *Through These Gates: Linwood Park*. (Haddonfield, NJ, 1984).

Brown, Jeffery D., and Raymond D. Fete. *Meyers Lake Park Remembered*. (Canton, OH, 1993).

Bush, Lee O., Edward C. Chukayne, Russell Allon Hehr, and Richard F. Hershey. *Euclid Beach Park Is Closed for the Season*. (Cleveland, 1977).

——. *Euclid Beach Park—A Second Look*. (Mentor, OH, 1979).

Francis, David W. "Cedar Point and the Characteristics of Summer Resorts During the Gilded Age." *Hayes Historical Quarterly* 7 (Winter 1988): 5–27.

——. "The Forgotten Sisters: Passenger Transit to a Great Lakes Resort, 1895–1901." *Telescope* 27 (July–August 1978): 95–100.

——, and Diane DeMali Francis. *Cedar Point*. (Chicago, 2004).

——. *Cedar Point: The Queen of American Watering Places*. (Fairview Park, OH, 1995).

——. *Chippewa Lake Park*. (Chicago, 2004).

——. *Luna Park: Cleveland's Fairyland of Pleasure*. (Fairview Park, OH, 1996).

——. *The Golden Age of Roller Coasters*. (Chicago, 2003).

——. *Ohio's Amusement Parks*. (Chicago, 2002).

——. *Summit Beach Park: Akron's Coney Island*. (Akron, OH, 1993).

LeDuc, Blake. *Euclid Beach Park Yearbook*. (Eastlake, OH, 1996).

Shale, Rick, and Charles J. Jacques, Jr. *Idora Park: The Last Ride of Summer*. (Jefferson, OH, 1999).

Photo Credits

4–9, author

10, top right, The Humphrey Company; bottom left, author

11, top right, The Humphrey Company; bottom left, author

12, Library of Congress

13, top left, Library of Congress; bottom right, author

14–20, author

21, top, CSU; bottom, author

22, author

23, top right, The Humphrey Company; bottom left, author

24–34, author

35, CSU

36, Amusement Park Books

37, top, Cleveland Public Library; bottom right, James Abbate

38, Ohio Historical Society

39, top, Western Reserve Historical Society; bottom, Amusement Park Books

40, Library of Congress

41, top Amusement Park Books; bottom, author

42, Cleveland Public Library

43, top left, author; bottom right, CSU

44, top, Western Reserve Historical Society; bottom, author

45, top left, Cleveland Public Library; bottom, Cleveland Plain Dealer

46, Amusement Park Books

47, top, Amusement Park Books; bottom, CSU

48, top right, author; bottom, CSU

49, CSU

50, Cleveland Plain Dealer

52, Cleveland Plain Dealer

53, Case Western Reserve University

54, CSU

55–72, Amusement Park Books

73–76, CSU

77, author

78, top right, CSU; bottom left, Amusement Park Books

79, top right, author; bottom, Amusement Park Books

80, Amusement Park Books

81, CSU

82, top left, Amusement Park Books; bottom, author

83, top, Amusement Park Books; bottom left, author

84–87, author

88, Amusement Park Books

89, top right, author; bottom left, Amusement Park Books

90–93, Joyce Biddulph

94, Amusement Park Books

95, top left, Amusement Park Books; bottom, CSU

96, CSU

97, Don Woodward

98, Cleveland Public Library

99, top left, Lake County Historical Society, bottom, CSU

100, Cleveland Public Library

101–103, author

104, top left, Lakewood Historical Society; bottom, author

105–107, Library of Congress

108, author

110, author

111–112, Memphis Kiddie Park Collection

113, CSU

114, top, CSU; bottom left, Memphis Kiddie Park Collection

115, author

116, Don Woodward

117–118, author

119, CSU

120–121, Don Woodward

122–124, CSU

125, top left, author; bottom, CSU

*CSU - Cleveland Press Collection, Cleveland State University Archives